Calvin's Ecclesiastical Advice

Calvin's Ecclesiastical Advice

John Calvin

Translated by
Mary Beaty and Benjamin W. Farley

Foreword by
John Haddon Leith

T&T CLARK
EDINBURGH

© 1991 Westminster/John Knox Press

Originally published in the United States of America by
Westminster/John Knox Press

This edition published under licence from Westminster/John Knox Press by

T&T Clark
59 George Street
Edinburgh EH2 2LQ
Scotland

First Published 1991

ISBN 0 567 29196 0

British Library Cataloguing in Publication Data
Calvin, Jean 1509–1564
Calvin's ecclesiastical advice.
1. Christianity. Theology
I. Title
230

Printed in the United States of America by
R. R. Donnelley & Sons Co.,
Crawfordsville, Indiana

In Gratitude for the Life and Work of

William F. Keesecker (1918–)
Presbyterian Pastor
Student of the life and work of John Calvin
Moderator of the General Assembly of the United
   Presbyterian Church in the United States of America, 1975

Lewis Bevins Schenck (1898–1985)
Davidson College Class of 1921
Professor of Bible, 1927–1966
J. W. Cannon Professor of Bible, 1941–1966

Ernest Albert Beaty (1898–1967)
Davidson College Class of 1921
Professor of Latin and German, 1925–1966
W. R. Grey Professor of Latin, 1960–1966

Contents

Foreword

The Colloquium on Calvin Studies, which has met at the Davidson College Presbyterian Church and Davidson College every two years since 1982, has demonstrated a wide interest in Calvin's theology among pastors as well as academicians. Members of the colloquium found in Calvin not simply an object of study but a source of guidance for the proclamation of the gospel today. They have shared an enthusiasm for the place of Calvin studies in the life of the church. They have been committed to conferences, to the publication of studies, and to the translation of Calvin material not available in English.

This book contains a collection of short articles in which Calvin gives his advice to individuals and to congregations about theology, ethics, worship, politics, economics, as well as church practices. These short articles, written for particular situations, demonstrate how Calvin applied the theology of the *Institutes* and the biblical exegesis of the commentaries to the issues of everyday life among individuals as well as congregations. They are therefore useful not simply for the understanding of Calvin's theology, but also as a guide for the Christian life in our time. They focus, as the Colloquium has attempted to do, on theology and practice.

The need for these writings and other Calvin material to be made available in English came to the attention of William F. Keesecker, pastor of the First Presbyterian Church, Oklahoma City, Oklahoma. William Keesecker himself had been a longtime student of Calvin and has published several Calvin anthologies. He has made use of Calvin's writings in his work as a preacher and churchman. At his request, William Keesecker and John Nichols of the Session of the First Presbyterian Church in Oklahoma City met at the Davidson Colloquium in 1988 with Keith Crim of The Westminster Press, John H. Leith, George Telford, Elsie McKee, and Brian Gerrish. This

group discussed which Calvin writings needed to be published
and how this was to be done. There was agreement in the discussion that the translation of Calvin's ecclesiastical advice
would serve a very useful purpose. After the meeting, John
Nichols took responsibility for raising funds to ensure the publication of four books in honor of the service of William
Keesecker as pastor of the First Presbyterian Church of Oklahoma City and former moderator of the Presbyterian Church.

We are fortunate to have two able translators. Dr. Mary Beaty
is Reference Coordinator and Assistant Director of the Library
at Davidson College. She is a scholar in classical literature, having taught in the Classics Department of the University of Richmond, and is an author, her latest book being *A History of
Davidson College.* Dr. Beaty has provided translations that are
not only exact but very readable. Dr. Roy Lindahl, Jr., of the
Department of Classical and Modern Languages of Furman
University, made an original translation of the Latin material,
but because of professional commitments was not able to bring
the translation to a finished stage. The French translations were
done by Benjamin W. Farley, who is Younts Professor of Bible
at Erskine College. He is a translator of Calvin's sermons as well
as of his tracts against the Anabaptists and the Libertines.

Dr. Charles Raynal, Pastor of the Davidson College Presbyterian Church, Davidson, North Carolina; Dr. James Goodloe,
Pastor of Gilwood Presbyterian Church, Concord, North Carolina; and Professor Farley helped write the introductions to the
documents. Professor Brian Armstrong, of Georgia State University, contributed generously of his time and talents to the
editing of the manuscript.

This volume is appropriately dedicated to William F.
Keesecker, whose great ministry in the church was enhanced by
his study of Calvin; and to Ernest Albert Beaty, father of Dr.
Mary Beaty; and to Lewis Bevins Schenck, who taught Benja-
min Farley at Davidson College. Professor Beaty and Professor
Schenck lived with the dignity of Christian faith and served
God in their vocations as Christian scholars and teachers in a
church college.

John H. Leith

Union Theological Seminary in Virginia

Translators' Preface

The documents in this collection, designated as *Calvin's Ecclesiastical Advice*, may be found in the *Corpus Reformatorum*, volume 38, part I. In this volume the *CR* editors have compiled forty-six of Calvin's writings, most of them letters, under the Latin title *Consilia*. Thirty-two are in Latin; fourteen are in French. Only eleven bear dates or indicate the day, month, or year of composition. Most list no designated receiver. Frequently a hand other than Calvin's has provided their titles. Most if not all were dictated; occasionally the secretary's name is mentioned. None of this simplifies the historian's task, but at the same time neither does it obscure the value or relevance of Calvin's advice.

The *CR* editors have grouped these pieces under seven general headings:

1. Dogmatics and Polemics
2. On the Changes and Need for Changes in Religion
3. Concerning the Worship of Images
4. On Ecclesiastical Discipline
5. Marriage Questions
6. Judicial Questions
7. Miscellanies

The largest number of documents are assigned to the section "On Ecclesiastical Discipline"; the second largest appear under "Dogmatics and Polemics."

The advice contained in these pieces portrays the familiar reformer whom Calvinists have come to know and expect, occasionally surprising his readers with the depth of his compassion and wit, patience and rigor. All display him as a counselor fully conscious of the sensibilities he will evoke and provoke, as a discerning historian and exegete, often as a reluctant but stalwart polemicist, as a theologian committed to the apostolic and catholic explication of the faith, and as an ever knowledgeable realist with regard to the political, social, moral, and economic conditions of his time.

The documents are of interest not only because they preserve what Calvin has to say but because they contain his justifications for what he believes to be the Christian and biblical way of being and doing. Thus, in the process of suggesting what course of action one might pursue, Calvin also provides his rationale, often citing his favorite patristic sources.

Any comprehensive assessment of Calvin's ecclesiastical advice cannot be based on a reading of the documents in this collection alone. That assessment must also include an examination of Calvin's *consilia* found throughout his *Institutes*, and in his sermons, commentaries, treatises, and letters.

The translators are grateful to John H. Leith, who coordinated the various aspects of the project.

PART I

Dogmatics and Polemics

1. Regarding the Name of God and Its Use in Prayer

The *CR* editors identify Jean Paul Alciati as the recipient of this letter. No date is given. In conjunction with this letter, see Calvin's Commentaries—in particular, his analysis of John 14:13–14, 17. See his comments on John 16:26; as well as on Hebrews 7:23; 1 John 2:1; and Romans 7:34. See also *Institutes* 3.20.17ff. (2:874ff.). [*CR* 38/I, pages 153–155]

When we speak of God alone, without adding further to his name, we should think of him in his pure essence as one sole God.

When we speak of Jesus Christ alone, without mentioning the Father, we ought to perceive him as God manifest in the flesh. We may justify this on the grounds that God has assumed our nature in order to indwell it as he would his own majestic temple, but in such a way that Jesus Christ, both in his divine essence and human nature, constitutes one singular person.

However, whenever we speak of God and Jesus Christ together, then we are referring to both the Father and the Son, who is the Lord and head of the church, whom the Father has ordained to rule over us and to exercise complete preeminence in his name.

In any case, whenever we think of God or want to speak of him, we ought to avoid dwelling on his infinite essence. This form of thinking is dangerous, since human understanding becomes confused by it. Rather, we should constantly return to Jesus Christ, in whom the Father has revealed himself to us.

When we refer to the scriptures, we ought to distinguish between the Old and the New Testament. For example: The Law and the Prophets proceed from Jesus Christ, insofar as he has always been the supreme Angel and the principal ambassador through whom God communicates to men. Nonetheless, the common practice was not to say that this [particular passage] was said by Moses or that [one] by David, but simply to say that God said these things. This was due to the fact that Christ had not yet appeared at that time.

For this reason we ought readily to believe, in accordance with St. Peter's teaching, that all the holy prophets spoke by the

Spirit of Jesus Christ and, in accordance with St. Paul's teachings, that he was Israel's guide and that even the law was given
by his hand. Nevertheless, following the accepted style of the
scriptures, when referring to things in the Old Testament we do
not say that Jesus Christ said them through the mouth of Isaiah
or Moses, but we say that God thus spoke or even his Spirit
[thus spoke].

With regard to the New Testament, there is another reason
[why we ought to believe that it proceeds from Christ]. For in
Christ's coming into the world the Father ordained him to be
our teacher and master for the purpose of declaring all truth to
us. Hence, we should both regard and call him Author of all
that the apostles teach, as St. Paul himself does.

As for prayers, whether we are invoking God without expressly mentioning Jesus Christ, or are requesting the Father to
hear us by virtue of his Son (whom we present as our mediator), or are addressing our prayer directly to him—if we do not
actually utter by mouth the name of Christ, we ought to be
thinking about it in our minds. Not because we are required at
all times to think that we can only approach the Father by
means of his Son's advocacy, but because we ought to possess
at all times the fundamental and principal realization that our
only access to God in prayer consists in being brought before
his majesty by him who humbled himself to our level in order
to accommodate himself to our littleness.

When we entreat the Father by name, requesting him to hear
us in the name of his Son, we ought to keep in mind that it is
our Lord Jesus, through the sacrifice of his death, who has won
the entrance for presenting us boldly to God, and that by virtue
of this sacrifice he intercedes for us, making it possible for our
prayers to be acceptable to God and for us to obtain our requests. Nor ought we to imagine that Christ does this by making supplications on his knees in the manner of men. But let us
be content to accept him as an advocate, as one who carries the
word in our name, and as one who receives our prayers in
order to present them to God and to obtain a favorable audience for us.

I say "audience," insofar as God permits and grants us liberty
to call upon him and listens to us. I say "favorable," insofar as
he grants us, by his grace, what we ask him. Consequently, the
following ought to be the attitude of every Christian who prays
to God in the name of his Son: "If I should be required to go

before God without any guide or intermediary, I would never be able to come before his majesty, for it is too high. But because I have the promise of my Savior, who holds my hand, my access to God becomes an easy matter."

But one might be tempted to ask: "How is it that our Lord Jesus, who is God, is able to intercede with God?" For it would seem that he is praying to himself, which is contrary to reason.

To avoid this conclusion, two considerations must be held in conjunction. The first is that, although there is only one sole God, there is nevertheless in this single Divinity the distinction between the Father and the Son, of which we have spoken. Hence, there is nothing contradictory about our praying to the Father in particular, or our addressing ourselves explicitly to him.

The second is that our Lord Jesus, since he has assumed human flesh in order to accomplish our redemption, intercedes for us as mediator and advocate in accordance with that nature which he shares in common with us. Hence, whether we address our prayers to Jesus Christ or ask him to go with us to the Father as our mediator, and thereby to prepare the way for our coming to the Father, or whether we request him to help us by virtue of his uniqueness as the one to whom all power is given, in whom all the fullness of divinity dwells, and as the one eternal God who has been manifested in the flesh—either way is acceptable and godly.

2. On Sin and Redemption

This is a very brief treatment of the topics. A much fuller discussion may be found in Calvin, *Institutes,* Book 2, "The Knowledge of God the Redeemer in Christ, First Disclosed to the Fathers Under the Law, and Then to Us in the Gospel," especially chapters 1–5 (1:241ff.), on sin, and chapters 6–17 (1:340ff.), on redemption. [Pages 156–157]

The first man was created by God with an immortal soul and a mortal body. God adorned him with his own likeness so that he was free of any evil, and commanded him to enjoy everything in his pleasant garden except the fruit of the tree in which all life lay hidden. God was so anxious that man should keep his hands from this tree that he told him he would die on the very day he touched its fruit. He did touch it, however, and immediately died and ceased to be like God. This was the origin of death, as is shown by the words, "As often as you eat of it you will die." He ate it because he was deceived, as the next passage in Genesis shows. The words of the Hebrew wise man attest this as well: "Death entered the world through the ill will of the devil" (Wisdom 2:24). Paul agrees with this in several passages.

Man was driven into exile, therefore, with all his descendants so that, since he had lost the horn of plenty, he should be unhappy and undergo all sorts of labor and trouble and seek food for himself, sweating and enduring cold, often hungry, often thirsty, always wretched. At last God took pity on this unfortunate and altogether unhappy man; although he declared that the sentence he had pronounced on him was valid, he nevertheless gave his only and greatly loved son as a sacrificial victim to expiate man's great evil. By this amazing and unexpected compassion God showed his love for us much more clearly than if he had rescinded his sentence.

Christ, therefore, the Son of God, was conceived by the overshadowing of the Holy Spirit and was born of a virgin. At the last he was lifted on a cross and, by his own death, saved the human race from eternal death. From this came the first resurrection to life. John did not hesitate to say in the Apocalypse (Rev. 20:6) that the blessed share in this resurrection, and he says in the fifth chapter of his Gospel (v. 24) that they "have passed from death to life."

The person who places all his hope of salvation in the cross of Christ will have no share in the second death, since he shares in the first resurrection, but anyone who scorns God's great kindness will have Christ as the judge of his impious and arrogant scorn rather than as a redeemer from universal destruction. This judgment by Christ, not of universal wrongdoing but of each person's individual misdeeds, will have the force of a second death. This will be, therefore, the origin of the second death.

John Calvin.

3. A Brief Admonition on the Lord's Supper

This document takes up the question of the relationship between the sign and the reality signified in the Lord's Supper. Of
course, Calvin argues that the reality of Christ's presence in the
Supper is received spiritually, not physically. A fuller discussion
may be found in the *Institutes* 4.17.1–50 (2:1359ff.), on "The
Sacred Supper of Christ, and What It Brings to Us." See also
4.14.1–26 (2:1276ff.), "The Sacraments"; and 4.18.1–20
(2:1429ff.), "The Papal Mass, a Sacrilege by Which Christ's
Supper Was Not Only Profaned but Annihilated." See also his
"Short Treatise on the Lord's Supper" (1541), in *Calvin: Theological Treatises,* trans. J. K. S. Reid, pp. 140–166; or "Short
Treatise on the Supper of Our Lord," in *Tracts and Treatises,*
trans. Henry Beveridge, vol. 2, pp. 163–198. See also Calvin's
"Essay on the Lord's Supper" from *The Form of Prayers,* 1542
and 1545, in Appendix I, below. [Pages 157–158]

There is general agreement that the Holy Supper represents
the communion which the faithful have with Christ. This is not
a subject of controversy.

A question has arisen, however: Is Christ, in the Supper,
merely giving an outward sign that we share in his body and
blood, or is he in fact fulfilling and keeping his promise that we
will share in his body and blood in such a way that he becomes
totally ours, and that by virtue of that communion all his bless-
ings extend to us?

We feel and we teach that the representation is real and that
therefore what is promised by a visible sign is made known
effectually in the Supper. This must mean that the faithful,
when they receive the sign, are sharing in the Lord's body and
blood; this is what it means to have the reality of the sign.

To avoid ambiguity we should define what it means to share
the Lord's body and blood. It is not simply to believe but to
receive Christ in faith in such a way that he dwells and remains
in us and that we become one body with him. Paul teaches that
we are flesh of his flesh and bone of his bones.

When we want to explain this, we say that it happens spiritually, and we interpret the word "spiritually" to include two
meanings: first, that this is the miraculous work of the Holy

Spirit, which exceeds the grasp of our minds (just as Paul, seized by wonder, exclaims that this is a great mystery); and secondly, that the eating does not take place in a fleshly way, with the body being broken into pieces by the teeth or swallowed by the mouth or going down into the stomach.

In this way we exclude all those absurd fantasies with which the world is preoccupied, fantasies about the presence of Christ in a certain place, or the scattering about of his glorified body. We do not conceive that Christ's presence in the Supper is of a sort to attach him to the element of the bread, or to enclose him in the bread, or in any way to circumscribe him. This would clearly diminish his heavenly glory. And we certainly do not conceive it as depriving him of his own dimensions, or pulling him apart into several places at once, or inventing for him an immense size. This would clearly be inconsistent with the reality of his human nature.

These qualifications must be explained carefully to the people, for we see that men are not concerned enough about true faith, by which alone we come into Christ's presence and remain close to him. They think they have Christ sufficiently present with them if they have his fleshly presence, which they dream up from sheer superstition, going beyond scripture. We also see the idolatry into which the world has fallen.

4. On Certain Somewhat Unleavened Points of Doctrine

This letter was written in response to an inquiry from some Christians apparently being "driven" about and almost compelled to subscribe to a confession of faith with which Calvin strongly disagreed. His criticisms and suggested revisions are clearly set forth here, particularly in regard to the sacraments. Additional material on these may be found in the *Institutes* 4.14.1–26 (2:1276ff.), "The Sacraments"; 4.15.1–22 (2:1303ff.), "Baptism"; 4.16.1–32 (2:1324ff.), "Infant Baptism Best Accords with Christ's Institution and the Nature of the Sign"; and 4.17.1–50 (2:1359ff.), "The Sacred Supper of Christ, and What It Brings to Us." [Pages 158–160]

Dearest brothers, your letter was delivered to us in the fourth month after it was sent, so you ought not to be surprised that you are receiving our answer to it more slowly than you had expected.

To come directly to the point, it grieves us deeply that you are being driven here and there, and that wherever you step, Satan is devising some way to cause you new troubles. The Fathers were in the same situation, as Paul testifies when he says that he and the other faithful wandered about with "no certain dwelling place" [1 Cor. 4:11].

Therefore, although you may often have to change the place you live and everything relating to your physical life, you must nonetheless learn true stability of mind and constancy of spirit. You must apply to yourselves the teaching that the sons of God must wander as strangers in the world. This applies to all the pious, although the Lord may wish some to experience it rather than others, as he leads them here and there. We are distressed for you and wish with all our hearts that we had some means at hand to end your unrest.

Nevertheless, our sympathy for your unhappiness does not allow us to free you from your responsibility. To do so would be nothing but to deceive you with empty flatteries and would not be useful for you. You know that God condemns us all the more when we are eager to be acquitted by men. Therefore we are going to tell you, clearly and simply, how we feel about your proposal.

In the first place, we were amazed to hear that you found nothing directly inconsistent with the Word of God in that confession which is demanded of you. We assume your eyes were blinded by fear. The section on baptism expressly condemns those who think that infants are sanctified from the time of their birth; and, as to the Supper, they say that Judas shared in the body of Christ no less than Peter. Likewise they say that Christ in his human nature can be anywhere he likes, since he is God and man, as if the unity of person caused a confusion of his divine and human nature.

You excuse yourselves by saying that it is not really a confession of faith, but (begging your pardon) this is nothing but a way to disguise and conceal evil. The Lord is no Sophist, to let himself be deceived by that sort of quibbling. Whatever name or term you use for that written statement, nonetheless you are bearing witness with a solemn oath that this is what you believe. Granted that the oath may not be carried all the way up to God, but by swearing in this way you are being double-tongued before men, and you cannot escape the disgrace of faithlessness. Granted, too, that those who proposed to you the terms of the confession did so with good intentions, it is not enough to strive for an upright purpose if you are using unlawful means.

We beg of you in the Lord's name to wake up if you have been lulled to sleep for a while. Let us state the case frankly: A written statement of that sort cannot be accepted without its indirectly renouncing the truth of God, and this truth should be dearer to us than any place to live, and dearer than life itself.

Here is the solution. You should substitute the words: "Baptism is not unnecessary for infants even though they are sanctified by promise." The sacrament is a confirmation that human weakness makes necessary; the promise brings the sacrament with it as a companion and certainly does not cause contempt for it.

In the section on the Supper, substitute this: "The substance of the true body and blood of Jesus Christ, as he received it from the Virgin's womb, is present in the Supper as much for the faithful as for the unfaithful." Only the faithful perceive it in actuality and effectually, but the unfaithful are no less answerable for the body and blood of the Lord because they defile the sacrament.

In place of the words "We reject the teaching of those who say that Christ is not perceived except in a spiritual way," you may substitute: " . . . of those who say that Christ is not perceived except as a spirit, with flesh and blood undoubtedly excluded." For it is written: "My flesh is meat indeed, and my blood is drink indeed" [John 6:55]. Although that perception is of a spiritual sort, it nonetheless takes place in actual fact and does not exist only in imagination or conjecture.

In place of the words "Christ is seated in accordance with his human nature," substitute: "We acknowledge that Christ is in heaven in accordance with his human nature, and we expect him to come from there; nevertheless, in accordance with his infinite virtue which extends everywhere, he can feed us with his body and blood in an incomprehensible way from the place where he sits at the right hand of the Father, without any change of place."

Where there is mention of *sacramentarii,* the word should be interpreted to mean those who either destroy the force of the sacraments or corrupt their use.

5. A Reply to Certain Questions of Laelius Socinus of Siena

Ford Lewis Battles notes that when Calvin writes in the *Institutes* against "certain perversely subtle men . . . who cannot bear to hear the word 'merit,' for they think it obscures God's grace," he is "presumably referring to Laelius Socinus (d. 1562)" (note on 2.17.1; 1:528). Battles then refers to this "Reply" (June 5, 1555) and further notes that "the questions of Socinus are not extant but can be inferred from Calvin's replies." He translates the first two sentences as follows: "It is a common rule that things subordinate are not opposed. Therefore, there is nothing to prevent the free justification of men out of the mere mercy of God from being accompanied by the merit of Christ." This whole chapter of the *Institutes,* "Christ Rightly and Properly Said to Have Merited God's Grace and Salvation for Us," would be of interest in regard to the first reply; see 2.17.1–6 (1:528ff.). In regard to the second, third, and fourth questions, see especially 2.2.6 (1:262ff.) and perhaps 3.2.1–43 (1:542ff.). See also 3.25.6–8 (2:996ff.), chapters that appear to be written against the view of Socinus "that the soul would be given a new body at the resurrection" and that are drawn largely from another letter from Calvin to him in June 1549. See George Huntston Williams, *The Radical Reformation.* [Pages 160–165]

Reply to the first question

It is a common rule that things which are ambivalent do not contradict one another. The justification of men can be, therefore, the undeserved result of God's pure compassion, and at the same time there can be a place in it for Christ's merit. God's undeserved favor is as much a contrast to our deeds, therefore, as is Christ's obedience; each has its own place. Christ could be of merit because it was pleasing to God, and because he was ordained to appease the anger of God by his sacrifice and to destroy our transgressions by his obedience. In a word, since Christ's merit depends altogether on God's compassion, which established this means of salvation for us, his merit is in contrast to all human righteousness no less properly than is God's compassion.

PROOFS

"God so loved the world that he gave his only begotten son, that whoever believes in him should not perish" [John 3:16]. We see that God's love holds the first place, as the highest cause or source. Faith in Christ follows as the second, and closely following, cause. If anyone takes exception to this and says that Christ is only a cause in a theoretical sense, this would diminish his virtue too much. If we attain righteousness by a faith that rests on him, then the means of our salvation must be sought in him. Many passages show this clearly: "Not that we first loved him but that he first loved us, and sent his Son as a propitiation for our sins" [1 John 4:10]. These words clearly show that God established in Christ the means of reconciliation, so that nothing should get in the way of his love for us.

The word "propitiation" carries great weight, for God, in some ineffable way, loved us and at the same time was angry with us until he was reconciled in Christ. All these statements relate to that: "He is the propitiation for our sins" [1 John 2:2]; and "It pleased God to reconcile all things to himself through him, having made peace through the blood of his cross," etc. [Col. 1:20]. Likewise, "God was in Christ reconciling the world to himself, not imputing their sins to men" [2 Cor. 5:19]; "He made us accepted in his beloved Son" [Eph. 1:6]; and "So that he might reconcile both unto God in one body by the cross" [Eph. 2:16].

The meaning of this mystery in the first chapter of Ephesians should be sought in the later passage, where Paul teaches that we were chosen in Christ and adds that we received grace in him. How did God begin to embrace with his favor those whom he had loved before the world was founded? He revealed his love only when reconciled by Christ's blood.

God is the source of all righteousness and therefore must be the enemy and judge of sinful man. Righteousness is the beginning of love, therefore, as Paul describes it: "He made him to be sin for us although he knew no sin, so that we might be the righteousness of God in him" [2 Cor. 5:21]. Paul means that we received undeserved justice through Christ's sacrifice, so that we might please God even though we are by nature "children of wrath" and alienated by sin [Eph. 2:3].

Many passages of scripture show, definitely and firmly, that Christ obtained his Father's grace for us by his obedience and is therefore well deserving. Paul is a witness that we were reconciled and gained reconciliation through Christ's death [Rom. 5:10], and there is no place for reconciliation unless there has been an offense. Therefore the meaning is this: God, to whom we were hateful because of our sin, has been propitiated by the death of his Son and has become gracious toward us.

We should be careful to note the antithesis that comes a little later: "For as by one man's disobedience many were made sinners, so by the obedience of one shall many be made righteous" [Rom. 5:19]. He means that just as we were alienated from God by Adam's sin and were destined for destruction, so by Christ's obedience we are received into his favor as if we were righteous. The future tense of the verb does not exclude present righteousness, as the context makes clear, for Paul had said earlier that grace was a means of justification from many sins.

When we say that we received grace by Christ's merit, we mean that we were washed clean by his blood and that his death was the expiation for our sins. "His blood cleanses us from all sin" [1 John 1:7]. This blood is poured out for remission of sins. If the result of this pouring out of his blood is that our sins are not imputed to us, it follows that the judgment of God was satisfied by this payment. John the Baptist's words refer to this: "Behold the Lamb of God, who takes away the sins of the world" [John 1:29]. He contrasts Christ to all the sacrifices of the law, to teach that he alone was the fulfillment of that figure of speech. We know that Moses says in many passages that iniquity will be expiated and that sin will be wiped out and remitted. In short, the early passages of figurative language teach us best how strong and effective the death of Christ is.

The apostle sets this matter forth skillfully in the letter to the Hebrews, taking as his starting point that remission of sins does not take place without the shedding of blood [Heb. 9:22]. From this he concludes that Christ came to destroy sin by his sacrifice once and for all and was offered up to take away the sins of many. The apostle had also said earlier: "Neither by the blood of goats and calves but by his own blood he entered in once into the holy place, having obtained eternal redemption." And he concludes: "If the blood of a calf sanctifies and purifies the flesh, how much more shall the blood of Christ purge your conscience from dead works?" [Heb. 9:13ff.]. In this passage he easily shows that we diminish Christ's grace too much if we do not acknowledge that his sacrifice had the power to expiate, propitiate, and give restitution. As he adds a little later [v. 15], "And for this cause he is the mediator of the new testament, that by means of death, for the redemption of the transgressions that were under the first law, they which are called might receive the promise of eternal inheritance."

It is especially helpful to examine the analogy that Paul uses: "Being made a curse for us," etc. [Gal. 3:13]. It was pointless and even absurd for Christ to be burdened with a curse unless, by paying what others owed, he gained righteousness for them. Isaiah's testimony is also clear [53:4, 5]: "The chastisement of our peace was upon Christ, and by his bruises we are healed."

If Christ had not made restitution for our sins he would not be said to have propitiated God by taking on himself the punishment we deserved. The passage that follows relates to this: "For the transgression of my people was he stricken" [Isa. 53:8]. In addition, there is Peter's interpretation, which leaves nothing unclear: "Because he bore our sins on the tree" [1 Peter 2:24]. He says that the burden of damnation was taken from us and put onto Christ. The apostles clearly state that he paid the price to redeem us from the condemnation of death: "Being justified freely by his grace through the redemption that is in Christ Jesus, whom God has set forth to be a propitiation through faith in his blood" [Rom. 3:25].

Paul commends God's grace, in that he gave the price of redemption in Christ's death, and he commands us to take refuge in that blood so that we may have righteousness when we stand before God to be judged. Peter's words are powerful: "Not redeemed by gold and silver but by the precious blood of the lamb without blemish" [1 Peter 1:18, 19]. His antithesis would not be appropriate if satisfaction had not been made for our sins by this payment. Therefore Paul says we were "bought with a price" [1 Cor. 6:20]. Another of Paul's statements, "There is one mediator who gave himself a ransom for all" [1 Tim. 2:5], would not hold true unless the punishment that we deserved had been laid on him. Therefore Paul defines redemption in the blood of Christ as remission of sins [Col. 1:14], as if to say that we are justified or absolved of guilt before God because that blood constitutes restitution.

Another passage agrees with this: "Blotting out the handwriting of ordinances that was against us" [Col. 2:14]. This passage notes the payment which absolves us from a state of guilt or counterbalances that guilt. There is also great weight in these words of Paul: "If righteousness comes by the law, then Christ died in vain" [Gal. 2:21]. We gather from this that we should seek from Christ the benefit that the law would confer if anyone could fulfill the law; or (and this amounts to the same thing) that we gain through the grace of Christ what God promised to our works in the law: "Which if a man do, he shall live in them" [Lev. 18:5]. What Paul says in a later passage relates to the same thing: "God sent forth his Son to redeem those who were under the law" [Gal. 4:5]. What does being under the law mean except that Christ gained righteousness for us by undertaking to be surety for the ransom we were not able to pay?

From this comes the imputing of righteousness without works, which Paul discusses in the fourth chapter of Romans, saying that the righteousness that is found in Christ alone has been transferred to us. For this reason, Christ's flesh is called our food [John 6:55], since we find in it the means of sustaining life. This strength comes only from the fact that the Son of God was crucified as the price of our righteousness. As Paul says, "He has given himself for us a sacrifice for a sweetsmelling savor" [Eph. 5:2]; and, in another passage, "He died for our sins and was raised again for our justification" [Rom. 4:25].

Not only is salvation given to us through Christ, therefore, but by his grace the Father is now favorable toward us. The saying which God pronounces figuratively through Isaiah is fulfilled in him: "For my own sake and for my servant David's sake" [Isa. 37:35]. The best witness of this is the apostle, who says, "Your sins are forgiven you for his name's sake" [1 John 2:12]. Although Christ's name is not mentioned, John nevertheless, according to his custom, designates him by the pronoun "his."

With the same meaning the Lord says: "As I live by the Father, so also you will live by me" [John 6:57]. Paul's saying corresponds to this: "For unto you it is given on behalf of Christ not only to believe on him but also to suffer for his sake" [Phil. 1:29].

Reply to the second question

Only those preordained for salvation are illuminated into faith and truly feel the effect of the gospel. Experience shows,

however, that the wicked are occasionally affected by a feeling
that is almost like the feeling of the elect, so that in their opinion they do not differ at all from the elect. It is not unreasonable that a taste of heavenly gifts and a temporary faith should
be given them. This happens not in order that they may feel the
force of spiritual grace and the definite light of faith, but because the Lord works his way into their minds to make them all
the more guilty and without excuse, since his goodness cannot
be tasted without the spirit of adoption.

Someone may object that the faithful have, therefore, no way
of being certain of their own adoption. My answer is this: Although there is a great likeness and affinity between God's elect
and those who are given a transient faith for a time, it is only in
the elect that the faith flourishes which Paul celebrates, saying
that they cry with a loud voice, "Abba, Father" [Rom. 8:15;
Gal. 4:6]. It is only the elect to whom God gives rebirth forever, with an incorruptible seed, so that the seed of life planted
in their hearts never perishes. He seals the grace of adoption in
them so firmly that it is lasting and valid. This by no means
prevents the inferior working of the spirit from taking its
course in the wicked. Meanwhile, the faithful are taught to
search themselves carefully and humbly so that reliance upon
the flesh does not creep in and replace the certainty of faith.

The wicked never have a sense of grace except in a confused
way; they see the shadow rather than the solid body. The spirit
seals remission of sins only in the elect, and in such a way that
they can apply it to their use with particular faith. It is for good
reason, however, that the wicked are said to believe that God is
favorably inclined toward them, since they have the gift of reconciliation, although in a confused and insufficiently distinct
way. They are not sharers with the sons of God in the same
faith or in rebirth, but they have with them a common starting
point.

I do not deny that God illumines the minds of the wicked so
that they perceive his grace, but he distinguishes that feeling
from the unique testimony that he gives his elect; consequently
they do not come to real completion and fruition. He does not
show himself favorable toward them in order to snatch them
from death and receive them into his keeping, but shows them
a compassion only for the present. He considers that only the
elect are worthy of the living root of faith, so that they may
persevere to the end. This refutes the objection that God's

grace, if once truly shown, is permanent and lasting. Nothing prevents God from illuminating some with a present sense of his grace, which afterward vanishes away.

Reply to the third question

Faith in the divine will toward us is something that can be known, and our persuasion of its truth is certain. Nonetheless, it is not surprising that the sense of divine love vanishes when it is given only for a time. Granted that this sense is related to faith; it differs from it greatly. I believe that the will of God is unchanging and that his truth always remains constant, yet I deny that the wicked progress so far that they enter into the revelation that scripture claims for the elect alone. I deny that they receive God's will in a permanent way or embrace his truth with constancy; they rest in a feeling that is transitory. They are like a tree that is not planted deeply enough and that will dry up with the passage of the seasons, even though it may send down living roots and put out flowers and leaves for several years, and even bear fruit.

In short, just as the first man's rebellion could wipe the image of God from his mind and spirit, so we should not be surprised that God illumines the wicked with certain rays of his grace, but afterward allows the rays to be extinguished. He is free to touch some people lightly with a knowledge of his gospel while imbuing others with it deeply.

We must hold to this: However small and weak the faith of the elect may be, the Spirit of God is nonetheless a sure guarantee for them, and the seal of their adoption, and a sculpted image that can never be blotted out of their hearts. The wicked, on the other hand, are touched here and there with a light that afterward perishes. The Spirit is not deceitful, however, even though he does not give life to the seed that he places in their hearts or cause it to remain incorruptible and everlasting, as in the case of the elect.

Reply to the fourth question

The teaching of scripture and our own everyday experience make it clear that the wicked are sometimes touched by a sense of divine grace and naturally feel some longing for a mutual love. Saul felt a strong sense of piety for a time, so that he loved

God, who had treated him in a fatherly way, and was capti-
vated by the charm of his goodness. But just as God's fatherly
love is not firmly rooted in the wicked, so they in turn do not
love him in a firm way but only out of mercenary desires, so to
speak. Only to Christ was the spirit of love given in such a way
that he instills it into those who are parts of his body.

Paul's saying is open only to the elect: "The love of God is
shed abroad in our hearts by the Holy Ghost which is given
unto us" [Rom. 5:5]. This is the love which produces that confident prayer which I have mentioned above.

I declare also that although God does not cease to love his
sons, he is amazingly angry with them, not because he hates
them but because he wants to frighten them with an awareness
of his anger, to humble their pride in the flesh, to shake them
out of their torpor, and to arouse them to repentance. His sons,
therefore, realize that he is angry with them (or, rather, with
their sins), and at the same time they realize that he is propi-
tious toward them. They sincerely pray that his anger may
pass, and yet they flee to him with calm confidence.

6. Against Osiander

Calvin clearly disagrees at many points with Andreas Osiander
(1498–1552), a prominent Lutheran pastor and leader of the Reformation in Nuremberg until 1549, when he became professor at
Königsberg. The subject of this writing is justification by faith,
about which he also argues with Osiander in the *Institutes*
3.11.1–12 (1:725ff.). See also 1.15.3–5 (1:186ff.); 2.12.5–7
(1:469ff.); and Index II (2:1622), which gives a number of other
references to Osiander. [Pages 165–167]

He could have been helpful to the church of God if he were
moderate, but when he is burning to show his cleverness, no
religious feeling or moderation or even shame restrains him
from trying to overthrow everything. He has corrupted the genuine and simple teaching of piety by perverse fantasies while
indulging in his own speculations. But I will not touch on his
other falsehoods now.

In explaining justification by faith, he has bewitched himself
with pure illusions and has deluded others. He admits what he

does not dare to deny, that remission of sins intervenes in the justifying of a person. But he places the image of the essence of righteousness at the first and highest level (an appearance that he has fashioned himself) and leaves nothing to the gracious acceptance of God, which he makes only a sort of inferior appendix. He has imagined this essence of righteousness for himself, on no rational basis. Although he draws on the testimony of scripture, which says that God dwells in us and that we are made one with him, this proves nothing except that, by the mysterious power of the Spirit, we are made one with God when we grow together into the body of Christ.

The idea of the essence of communion was taken from the ravings of the Manicheans. I do not see how he can justify the absurd idea that the essence of God's righteousness is a happenstance, present with a man one moment and absent the next. There is no need for a lengthy refutation if we hold to the basic fact that man's righteousness was an uprightness present at his very creation, and that he was shaped to this so that God's glory might shine forth in the separate parts of his soul and even in his body. Man was endowed with the light of intelligence and was disposed by his will to be obedient to God, and he had the same symmetry in each of his faculties; therefore we say that man was just. Osiander is not content with this description. He imagines that Christ was not only the Idea but the primary exemplar, so that Adam was essentially his image. This is the source of that falsehood on which he has become so drunk that he is not guarding himself against any absurdities.

After man was alienated from God, we say that he was restored by righteousness and by sanctification. The former means undeserved reconciliation; the latter means man's renewal. In his use of the words, Osiander falsely confuses regeneration with righteousness. Paul's saying holds good, that David gave a true definition of righteousness in the words "Blessed is the man to whom God does not impute iniquity" [Rom. 4:8].

Osiander says we are justified not only by the obedience that Christ showed and by the ransom he paid in dying to expiate our sins, but by his divine and eternal justice. Paul is very different. He simply affirms that we are justified by the obedience of one man [Rom. 5:19], and says in another passage that Christ was given for us for redemption and righteousness [1 Cor. 1:30]. He was "made under the law" to redeem us from the curse of the law [Gal. 4:4]. This, then, is the righteousness that Paul discusses in many passages: that we are received by God into grace, with our guilt wiped away. The words "For their sakes I sanctify myself" [John 17:19] certainly refer to the human nature of Christ. If Christ's flesh is truly our food and his blood truly our drink, we conclude that we are justified in him only because he is the propitiator.

One passage from Paul makes abundantly clear how ignorantly and perversely Osiander speaks about reconciliation: "God was in Christ reconciling the world to himself, not imputing their trespasses unto them" [2 Cor. 5:19]. We should also note the account of righteousness that Paul adds soon afterward: "For he has made him to be sin for us, who knew no sin, that we might be made the righteousness of God in him" [2 Cor. 5:21].

I hope this brief admonition will be enough to protect sensible and temperate readers against Osiander's illusions. I do not have time to write at length now, and I do not think it would be useful.

7. Against Menno

Menno Simons (1496–1561), leader of the Anabaptists in the Netherlands and the one from whom the Mennonites draw their name, also comes under attack by Calvin in the *Institutes* 2.13.1–4 (1:474ff.), a chapter entitled "Christ Assumed the True Substance of Human Flesh." There Calvin regards Menno as a contemporary Marcionite reviving an ancient heresy that denied the reality of Christ's body. To learn more about Menno Simons, see George Huntston Williams, *The Radical Reformation.* See also John Calvin, *Treatises Against the Anabaptists and Against the Libertines,* ed. and trans. Benjamin W. Farley (Grand Rapids: Baker Book House, 1982), and Willem Balke, *Calvin and the Anabaptist Radicals* (Grand Rapids: Wm. B. Eerdmans Publishing Co., 1982). [Pages 167–176]

Your letters do not weary me at all, dear brother; to be interrupted by them is welcome and pleasant. I only wish you had a happier subject so that I could share your joy. But since it pleases the Lord to trouble us, it should not be bothersome to write back and forth about your general concerns for the church. I wish I could help you as much as I would like to. At any rate, I will willingly give you all the support and assistance I can.

I have some acquaintance with Menno's teachings, which he drew from the ravings of the Manicheans, although I do not have a complete grasp of his fallacies. To oppose them we must acknowledge and set forth clearly, as I am sure you have done, that Christ is God manifest in the flesh, the true Son of God, and that although the word "son" is properly consistent with his divine nature and refers to it, nonetheless, as a human being, born of a virgin, he is also properly called "son." As mediator and head of the church, both God and man, he is the Son of God by nature, joining us to himself in the grace of adoption.

It is absurd to conclude from this, however, that as man he was born from his Father's seed. Christ in his entirety is truly called the Son as a result of a mysterious and sacred union of divinity with flesh. Paul makes this especially clear in the first chapter to the Romans [vs. 3 and 4] and in the ninth chapter [v. 5]. Regardless of Menno's quibbling, the sense is clear: that Christ is the Son of God from the seed of David according to the flesh; and that Christ, who is God and is blessed forever, is descended from the Jews according to the flesh. It is useless for Menno to seize upon passages where Christ as man is called the Son of God. The word "son" is properly conferred upon the entire person of Christ. When Christ is said to have come from heaven and to have gone out from the Father, this is wrongly interpreted to apply to the essence of his flesh. We can gather that Christ is truly God, but Menno proclaims this not so much on the basis of his substance as of his position, since he wants to assert that it means only that Christ is divine.

Menno wants to weaken the arguments that prove orthodox doctrine, but he slips about with nothing but silly quibbling. He says, for example, that if the Spirit could be changed into flesh (and with God all things are possible), then the Father too could be changed into flesh. If we grant this, what about the words "I fill heaven and earth"? [Jer. 23:24]. All divinity would then have to be one body, which would be contained in a single place. If Christ's body had been divine, he would have been wrong in saying that God is a spirit, and that after the resurrection the Spirit does not have flesh and bones.

I cannot imagine anything more absurd than Menno's argument that the Spirit was changed into flesh and ceased to be what it really was. This would mean that the eternal nature of the spiritual essence will die. Besides, if Christ is man from the seed of God (as Menno says), then God's essence is no longer unified and unmixed but is cut up into parts, and there is the sort of division in God which Menno does not acknowledge between the two natures of Christ.

As to his objection that otherwise the passage in John (that "the Word became flesh") is not true because the verb "became" does not mean simply "assume," this is nonsense. In the second chapter to the Hebrews [v. 14] the apostle is certainly not disagreeing with John when he uses the verb "assume." The meaning of this way of speaking is clear enough; someone who was a private citizen is said to "become" king because he begins to be something he was not. And so, truly and appropriately, the Son of God is said to have become flesh when he puts on flesh.

To say that Christ is called the Son of Man because he was promised to mankind is a disgusting attempt to avoid the issue, and Menno shows clearly enough by his lies that he is looking for ways to avoid it. It is clearly Jewish custom to call a human being "the son of man," and Christ certainly kept the vocabulary of his own language. The meaning of "the sons of Adam" should be beyond controversy. We do not need to go so far back, however. A passage in the Eighth Psalm [v. 4], which the apostles apply to Christ, ends all controversy: "What is man, that you are mindful of him, or the son of man, that you visit him?" As to Menno's nonsense about the masculine gender, this is a colorless argument; anyone whose origin is from Adam is called "the son of man."

Menno tries in vain to overturn the principle that the sins of the world must be expiated in our flesh. Paul clearly asserts this in the fifth chapter of Romans [vs. 10, 19]. As to Menno's objection that no one born of sinful flesh could fulfill the law, the answer should be sought in the eighth chapter of the letter to the Romans, verse 3, where Paul teaches that expiation was made "in the likeness of sinful flesh." We know that the nature of man was not corrupt from the beginning but became so from the occurrence of sin. What would prevent God, therefore, from being able to sanctify the flesh of his own Son?

This argument remains strong: If Christ was not born as a human being there was a new sort of creation. Menno says that new creations do not occur every time something is miraculously changed into a new nature, but this is a violent twisting [of the argument]; God's essence could not be changed the way a creature's could, and it is a detestable lie to imagine that God's essence is spirit in the Father but body in the Son.

Menno impudently leaps over the argument drawn from the sharing of gifts. Whatever the Father has bestowed upon Christ surely pertains to us, since Christ is the head from which the whole body is fastened together and grows into one. Otherwise there is no meaning to the words "The Spirit is given to him without measure, so that we might all drink of his fullness" [John 1:16; 3:34], unless it does not seem absurd to Menno for God to be enriched in his own being by a gift from outside himself. Christ himself says on this subject: "For their sakes I sanctify myself" [John 17:19], and Menno is lying when he says this cannot be read anywhere in scripture.

If the testimony of Moses is examined well, it overwhelms Menno so completely that he cannot disentangle himself. Moses speaks not of Christ only but of the whole human race. It is true that the victory is won by Christ, but God declares in general terms that the descendants of a woman will have dominance over the devil [Gen. 3:15]. It follows from this that Christ was born of the human race. Menno's cabalistic allegories pervert the sense of this altogether. He says that "woman" means the church, but God's intent is to encourage Eve (whom he is addressing) and give her good hope. Menno's varied interpretations of this passage show that he is a twisting and slippery serpent himself, but when he says that victory over the serpent is promised and will come from a woman who is without seed, he cannot twist out of this in any way. If the woman was without seed, the promise would be false.

Menno wickedly corrupts the passages where Christ is called the seed of Abraham and the fruit of David's belly. If the word seed had been used allegorically, Paul would certainly have mentioned it in the fourth chapter of Galatians, verse 4. He affirms clearly, and with no figure of speech, that there are not many sons of Abraham who are redeemers, but only Christ. I acknowledge that in terms of genealogy Christ is not shown to be the son of David except as a result of being born of a woman. Menno, however, to strengthen his impious mistakes, arrogantly overturns the basic facts of nature by contending that women are without seed.

He gets around the eighth argument, about Christ's genealogy, in a sophistic way. Matthew surveys Joseph's parentage rather than Mary's, but, since he was writing about a matter commonly understood at the time, he is satisfied to show that Joseph was descended from David's seed, since it was well known that Mary was of the same family. Luke expresses this even more strongly when he teaches that a common salvation was brought by Christ to the whole human race because Christ, the source of salvation, was descended from Adam, everyone's common father.

Matthew makes it clear that Christ was created of Mary's seed because he was born of her. When Boaz is said to have been born of Rahab, this indicates a similar sort of bringing to life. Matthew is not describing the virgin as a channel, so to speak, through which Christ passed. He distinguishes this miraculous sort of procreation from the ordinary in that, through Mary, Christ was descended from the seed of David. Christ is said to have been born of his mother in the same way in which Isaac was begotten of Abraham, Solomon of David, and Joseph of Jacob. The gospel writer continues to use the traditional wording.

Menno shows his shamelessness in the tenth argument. How can he make these two things agree, that Christ is from the seed of David according to the flesh and yet that he is not called the Son except as he was promised and given? Paul named Christ as the Son of God and immediately added "of the seed of David according to the flesh" [Rom. 1:3], and therefore he is certainly noting something distinct from the divine being. In the ninth chapter, too [v. 5], speaking of Christ as God "blessed forever," he adds particularly that he was descended from the Jews "as concerning the flesh." If Christ were not really descended from the seed of David, what would that passage mean which says that he is the fruit of his belly and descended from his loins? Menno foolishly argues that Christ could not be called the natural son of David because the word was made flesh, but it is agreed that this is said only in the sense that Christ put on flesh and was manifest in the flesh.

Menno says that a woman does not have generative seed. Would anyone believe this figment of an ignorant man's imagination, contrary to everyone's common sense? It is surprising, though, that he denies a true miracle while inventing a totally false, extravagant story in which (if it were true) God's power would be even more amazing: namely, that God's eternal being was changed into a mortal body.

Menno argues that it cannot be taught definitely that Mary was born of the seed of David, but this is nonsense. When Matthew wanted to show that Christ was of David's seed, he was content to say that he was born of Mary, taking it as an accepted fact that Mary was related to Joseph by blood. As to Menno's saying that "seed" is used for "posterity," this is a weak argument. Christ is not simply called the seed, but is said to be from the seed. It is an intolerable degree of shamelessness to pervert the clear meaning in Paul's words and to say that Christ was not made or formed from David's seed.

Concerning Menno's eleventh argument, I acknowledge that "the church is spiritually flesh of Christ's flesh," etc. I say in turn, however, that in order for this to happen, Christ borrowed from men the flesh in which he was to sanctify himself on their behalf. It makes no sense to say that Christ is called heavenly from the word "heaven" because he brought his fleshly body from heaven. An antithesis clearly disproves this, for man is called both *terrenus* and *animalis,* and clearly his soul did not come from the earth. Therefore nothing is more certain than that Christ is called heavenly with respect to the life-giving spirit.

I do not deny that man's form as seen in the second chapter of Philippians [v. 7] is lowly and that his condition is low, but we can easily see from the total context that Christ emptied himself, taking the true nature of a man. Why does Christ wish to be in the appearance of a man, except that for a time the divine glory did not shine forth, but only a human form appeared? His exaltation [Phil. 2:9] pertains to this also; Christ is clearly said to have obtained new glory because he emptied himself.

However much Menno may twist the passage from the second chapter to the Hebrews, verse 11, he cannot disentangle himself from it. It says that the author of sanctification and those who are sanctified are all "of one," namely of God, and the context proves that a sharing of nature is to be understood. For the apostle adds immediately: "For which cause he is not ashamed to call them brethren." But if he had said earlier that the faithful were of God, what reason would there have been to feel shame in [the midst of] such worthiness? But Christ is said not to have felt shame because, out of immense grace, he joins himself to the lowly and ignoble. Menno objects in vain, saying that otherwise the impious would be the brothers of Christ. We know that the sons of God are born not of flesh and blood but of the Spirit through faith. The sharing of flesh alone does not produce brotherly communion.

He talks ignorant nonsense about "children," since the prophet, whose testimony the apostle is using, simply means "servants" or "disciples" [Isa. 8:17]. He babbles just as foolishly when he says that Mary would be the mother of her own brother if Christ is our brother according to the flesh. It is a common term in Hebrew for any relatives to be called brothers. Although the apostle bestows the honor of being one with Christ only upon the faithful, it does not follow that unbelievers are not born from the same origin. When we say that Christ was made man in order to make us the sons of God, this saying is not extended to everyone; faith is the intermediary that implants us in Christ's body in a spiritual way.

Menno argues impiously and wickedly when he says that Christ must have been born of Adam at the beginning, since he is the firstborn among brothers. Being the firstborn is meant to refer not to age but to level of honor and outstanding virtue.

The fifteenth argument is ignorant mockery. The apostle's words are clear: "As the children are partakers of flesh and blood, Christ likewise himself took part of the same" [Heb. 2:14]. As to what is said about human nature, Menno irrationally and shamelessly twists it to the point of sin. It is even worse that he limits the plural relative pronoun only to the flesh (and not genuine flesh, at that), as if the apostle were saying nothing in stating that Christ is a companion and sharer in the same nature with us. There is likewise no weight to his quibbling that Christ would be a sinner among sinners if he were truly a human. We do not concede that there was depravity of nature in Christ; we teach that he was created man without sin.

The passage from the second chapter of Hebrews [v. 16], in which the apostle says that Christ "took on him the seed of Abraham," refutes the impious lie of Menno and Servetus, who say that Christ received men into grace. The apostle magnifies the grace of which Christ considers the human race worthy by comparing angels to men, showing that Christ (think of it!) preferred men to angels since he put on the nature of men. If "seed" means "posterity," he will be forced to admit that angels have offspring, as if Christ lied when he said we would be like angels after the resurrection. Menno's subtlety about the present tense of the verb is futile; the apostle is making a point in his usual manner, to set this remarkable grace before our eyes more clearly.

Menno not only chatters ignorantly about the twofold nature in Christ but, by mixing everything up, even contradicts himself. Peter says that we will be "partakers of the divine nature" [2 Peter 1:4], but this can only refer to our being made new for heavenly glory. Otherwise our corruptible body would become God. How is it that Menno does not shudder at and abominate the change of sinful flesh into God's being, when he shrinks so violently from the thought that the Son of God has put on our flesh, which is not an unreasonable thing?

In addition, Peter thinks that sharing in the divine nature will destroy man's present nature insofar as it is weak. In Christ, moreover, there is a very different situation, since he is both God and man at the same time. If Menno attributes to Christ a human substance that is whole and strong, free of any stain, as Adam's was before the fall, then it follows that Christ's flesh was not born of the seed of God but of man, unless by chance he prefers to say that his flesh was created from nothing or from the earth. He finds fault with the saying of Athanasius that Christ consists of two natures as a man consists of soul and body, but he needs to show why such an apt comparison displeases him.

I am not surprised that Menno turns his back on the passage [1 Peter 3:18] where Peter says that Christ was dead in the flesh but was made alive by the Spirit. How can he explain it when Peter ascribes to the Spirit that goodness which Christ's flesh lacked? Paul overwhelms him even more when he asserts that Christ suffered in accordance with the weakness of the flesh [2 Cor. 13:4]; if Christ's flesh was divine, then divinity was weak. Another passage that relates to this is that "Christ bore our sufferings and afflictions, being made like us in all ways, except sin." If God's nature was subject to distress and fear, indeed to all our weaknesses, the sun would not be bright and all the orderliness of sky and earth would be a shapeless and fearful chaos.

When he attempts to prove that women do not have generative seed, Menno's babbling does not deserve to be refuted. I leave it to the medical doctors to deal with. I can refute, however, the futile reasoning he uses. He says, for example, that Onan the son of Judah poured out his seed on the ground, and that we do not read of a woman doing that. The rascal is amusing himself by uncovering women's pudenda, as it were! He argues that a man who ejaculates semen is said to be unclean, and he foolishly implies that an unclean flow has no relevance to women. By this reasoning, women would not have that innate uncleanness which only men were given circumcision to prevent.

In the seventh chapter of the book of Wisdom [Wisd. Sol. 7:2] the human race is said to have been "formed in blood from the seed of a man." On this basis Menno tries to ascribe blood to the woman, as if it were peculiarly hers; as if sperm were anything but blood shaped for the purpose of producing life. It follows from this that the fetus develops as much from a woman's substance as from a man's.

The rascal wickedly corrupts the passage where Paul teaches that "the man is not of the woman, but the woman of the man" [1 Cor. 11:8]. There is no doubt that Paul is discussing the beginning of the human race and not the continuing propagation of the race, which he mentions immediately in another part of the sentence where he says that man is "also by the woman" [v. 12].

When he argues that Aaron and Joiada took wives from the tribe of Judah, and concludes that the separation of the tribes would have ended if women had generative seed, this is a cold argument. We know how important it is for a state that children are counted as coming from a man's seed. The superior status of the male sex does not keep the woman's seed from uniting with the man's in the reproductive act. This explanation extends to all genealogies. When scripture reviews a list of people, it often names only men. Are we to say that therefore women are nothing? No. Even children know that women are included under the names of their husbands, because the name of a family always remains with the males.

He talks childishly about the mysterious nature of the church. Even though the church is called our mother, that does not mean that the individual parts correspond further in terms of fleshly and spiritual generation.

Creation does not show what Menno wants it to show, namely, that women are without seed. The first woman was created from a man, but all their descendants were created from them both. His reasoning based on the word "seed" is foolish. If a seed scattered by a man's hand takes root in the ground, it does not follow that the man's role has the same force in the sexual union of a man and a woman. We might rather argue that, because a mother was once called *genetrix,* a woman's seed works together with a man's for procreation. Otherwise, a niece's marriage to her mother's brother would have been wrongly forbidden by the law of God, since there would have been no blood relationship.

His reasoning is just as foolish when he says that children are judged noble or ignoble on the basis of their father's status. Although the male sex has this advantage, nonetheless, in cases of slavery the offspring follows the womb, as lawyers say. From this it is easy to gather that the fetus is conceived from its mother's seed.

Menno's conclusion is no less outlandish when he says that women would be the fathers of their fetuses if they contributed seed. But the mother is called the parent no less than the father is; they share the name "parent," and the only distinction in the words mother and father is one of gender.

His last argument melts away of itself. I acknowledge that women are assigned a passive role, but I assert that the same thing is preached about women as about men, without distinction. Christ is not said to have been made through a woman but "of a woman" [Gal. 4:4]. We can see that this dog Menno is barking shamelessly.

He asks in a mocking way if we are willing to say that Christ was born of the virgin's menstrual flow. I would like to ask him, in turn, whether Christ developed in his mother's blood, since Menno elsewhere does not deny that she fulfilled the functions of a mother.

His explanations do not overturn the testimony of scripture, in which seed is attributed to women. The same (or equal) condition does not apply to a woman as to the earth, and when someone is said to be of the seed of a woman, we cannot understand this to mean posterity. In the third chapter of Genesis the whole human race is called the seed of woman, in the sense that the woman truly has a part in procreation. The passage in the eleventh chapter of the letter to the Hebrews [v. 11] cannot easily be ignored either: "Sarah received strength to send forth seed." Clearly that word means that seed comes out of women, and there is an obvious play on the meaning of *parabolē* and the verb *lambanesthai.* As to what relates to Christ, the sole, unadorned promise that he should be said to have come forth from the loins of Abraham and David will not bring that about.

Menno tries to load us down with insulting absurdities, saying that if God's Word was not also his Son from the beginning, then God was not the father of the angels; and saying, nevertheless, that he had no mother before he was born. We, on the other hand, submit that Christ was a man born of Mary, and that he was no less the son of God than of man, though in a different respect. We do not imagine a twofold Christ as in Nestorius's image; we maintain that there is one person from two natures, so that he is truly God "manifest in the flesh" [1 Tim. 3:16]. If Menno rejects our teaching on this subject, then he is mocking Paul, whose words we are using.

He argues that the crucified Christ is the only begotten Son of God. We teach the same thing, but with the distinction that Christ clearly stated with his own mouth when he called his body a temple [John 2:19]. How may a temple be God himself, or the essence of God? We conclude therefore that [his body] is the dwelling place of the deity. A passage in Paul's writings relates to the same thing: "For in him dwells all the fullness of the Godhead bodily" [Col. 2:9].

He argues foolishly that if we say Christ is God and man, then Christ would be divided into God and man. It is not hard to destroy this argument. A distinction is not the same thing as a complete dividing into pieces. With great impudence he says that Christ would then be composed of a pure and an impure nature, one blessed and the other accursed. But Paul, writing that God "condemned sin in the flesh" [Rom. 8:3], sensibly calls us back to "the likeness of sinful flesh."

Menno reasons childishly that if Christ was born from his mother's seed through the mysterious working of the Spirit, then a woman's seed is not impure, only a man's. We do not believe that Christ was free from all stain because he was born only of a mother, but because he was sanctified by the Spirit so that the act of procreation should be pure and whole as it was before the Fall.

Menno then adds that all descendants of Adam, without exception, are confined under the power of sin, and that Christ could not be free from this universal law if he drew his origin from men. The antithesis that Paul uses in the fifth chapter of Romans easily explains this: As by one man sin entered into the world and, through sin, death, so grace has abounded in the grace of one man, Christ. It is likewise in 1 Corinthians 15:47. The corruption of Adam by the occurrence [of sin] does not prevent Christ from being born of Adam, pure and whole.

It is certain (and Menno's quibbling cannot get around it) that every time scripture tells us about Christ's purity it notes that he had the true nature of a man. It would be superfluous to say that God is pure; the sanctification that John speaks of [17:19] would have no place in a divine nature. Adam's seed is not to be seen as having a twofold nature, even though Christ received no contagion from it; the procreation of a man is not unclean and sinful in itself but through the occurrence [of sin], because of the Fall. It is not surprising that Christ, who restored wholeness, was free from the general corruption.

Menno chatters uselessly when he says that if Christ had been born of Mary's seed, then she would be both his father and mother. As if that birth, in which God showed a memorable example of his mysterious and incomprehensible power, ought to be judged by the general rule!

That axiom which he offers so boldly, that Mary was without seed, wins no approval because it is inconsistent with both philosophy and experience.

He argues that it is idolatry to worship God manifest in human flesh. We deny this. How arrogant he is to fetter us with his own opinions! As to his argument that Christ would be more Gentile than Jew if he had been born of Mary, because he would draw his ancestry through women from the Gentiles, this is as futile as his other arguments. It is as if having Ruth as his ancestress kept David from being considered the son of Abraham.

He argues absurdly that if the Word of God put on human flesh, it was therefore closed up in the narrow dungeon of an earthly body. This is pure shamelessness. Although the immense essence of the Word developed into one person with the nature of a man, we are not to imagine any closing up. The Son of God miraculously came down from heaven in such a way that he did not leave heaven. He was willing to be miraculously conceived in a virgin's womb and was willing to live on earth and to hang on a cross so that he might fulfill the world forever, just as from the beginning. It is profane ignorance to imagine that the Word was separated from the flesh even in death. I would like to find out from Menno how it happens that the essence of God, which heaven and earth cannot contain, was made a small body that lay hidden in a virgin's womb and in a tomb. Let him untie this knot if he can! How was God everywhere as a spirit and at the same time a palpable man on earth? I see clearly that nothing can be imagined more arrogant than this jackass, or more petulant than this dog.

8. If Christians Can Be Given a Plan for a General Council

This document illustrates Calvin's deep concern for the unity of the church and his respect for a council as a way to pursue that unity. Here he sets forth what would be required for the council to be free. Of interest is the proposed order of topics— doctrine, worship, polity—as well as the particulars under each. See Calvin's letter (1552) to Thomas Cranmer (d. 1556), Anglican archbishop of Canterbury, on ecumenical councils, in *Letters of John Calvin,* ed. Jules Bonnet, vol. 2, pp. 345–348, where Calvin states, "So much does this concern me, that, could I be of any service, I would not grudge to cross even ten seas, if need were, on account of it" (p. 348). See *Letters of John Calvin,* vol. 4, pp. 158–161. See also "The Necessity of Reforming the Church" (1539), in *Calvin: Theological Treatises,* trans. J. K. S. Reid, pp. 183–216; or in *Tracts and Treatises,* trans. Henry Beveridge, vol. 1, *On the Reformation of the Church,* pp. 121–234. See also the *Institutes* 4.9.1–14 (2:1166ff.), "Councils and Their Authority." [Pages 176–178]

We need a free and general council to end the disturbances and disagreements by which we see the church being divided and torn. "Freedom" falls into three categories: the place, the persons taking part, and the manner or system of procedure.

As to the place, it is clear that the door to freedom will be closed unless there is safe access for all those who ought to be heard, so that they may debate controversial matters there. A city will have to be chosen that is central, therefore, and in the midst of all the regions from which the council participants will come. The neighboring princes who control the areas through which the participants will travel will need to promise and swear to give safe conduct for all who are convening.

As to the persons, it would be very unjust for the bishops alone to be allowed to give decisive judgments. We know quite well that their own cause will be taken up at the council, and they cannot be suitable judges of that cause. And then too, granted they have the authority which they claim, none of them is free; they are bound by an oath to obey the pope, and they are pledged to the Roman See, which is diametrically opposed to freedom.

It would be a suitable solution to appoint to the council men from the party that wishes and demands the reformation of the church, as much in its doctrine as in its mores. They would not have the decisive voice (as they say), but they would be free to intervene in any decrees and determinations that seemed inconsistent with the Word of God. They should be given a hearing, too, and their protests should be allowed. For their part, they should show that they have just reasons for contradicting and not agreeing with the bishops' opinions.

It is especially intolerable for the pope to preside over the council as its head, especially with this new qualification that everything depends on him and his judgment. He may have the place of honor (with everyone's permission), but reason demands that he should submit himself to the council in all matters, and should swear to observe whatever is decided there. He should give up the ruling power, which he has seized for himself, and become only one man among others. The bishops should also swear to obey the Word of God and to disregard their present status, and they should swear that they will not support or foster any corruptions that may be found in doctrine or in ceremonies or observances.

The procedure to be followed at the council would be a pitfall if the custom that has recently prevailed were to be kept: namely, that those who demand reformation have to explain their doctrine orally or in writing and that then, in their absence, the prelates decide what is permissible. All must be present, to correct anything the bishops want to decide on out of wickedness or ignorance. They must be free to oppose all mistaken opinions with clear and valid arguments.

It is very important to determine the order to follow. The articles of doctrine on which the parties disagree should be examined first; then the ceremonies should be dealt with, and then at the end, the governance of the church.

The chief points of doctrine that are debated today concern

the worship of God, whether it should be carried out in accordance with the sole and simple precept of scripture or whether men have the power and judgment to set laws to govern it and, by their traditional beliefs, to make souls liable to the punishment of death. Under this heading are prayers, prohibition of marriage, auricular confession, and similar matters. We must investigate and define where the faith of our salvation is founded: whether we are saved by the merit of works or by the undeserved compassion of God. Other questions depend on this: free choice, making reparation, purgatory, and similar matters. Invoking God in prayer is related to the certainty of faith and brings with it the question of the intercession of the saints.

In the second category, that of ceremonies, the council should debate the great mass of rituals that have been borrowed from the shadows of the law. At the same time it should consider the number of the sacraments and additions to them.

The third category, on the governance of the church, includes defining the office of bishop so that we may know which ones claim this title justly and deservedly. Other subjects relating to this are ranks, orders, the position of primates, and other similar matters.

If our purpose is to calm and soothe all the disturbances and quarrels that are troubling the church, it will not be sufficient merely to hold a council. It must be a universal council. Individual kings and princes can assemble a national council to find a solution to disturbances in their own realms, of course, even if their neighbors do not join them and add their consent and enthusiasm. But if we assemble only a partial council and call it universal, this will only inflame the fire, increase the combat, and create new disturbances. It is absolutely necessary that all who seek reformation should consent to the council that is to be held, so that all of Christendom may come together. Those who shrink from holy unity and concord are to be considered schismatics.

PART II

On the Changes and Need for Changes in Religion

1. A Letter Written in the Name of a Person Who Had Withdrawn from His Father Because of Religion

Here we find Calvin the pastor at work on an extremely personal and sensitive matter which nevertheless has much larger ramifications: a son has left the Roman religion of his father and embraced the Reformation. Calvin writes for him in a firm but peaceable way, seeking both to effect a reconciliation and to explain the faith. The emphasis here is placed upon worship according to the will of God as made known in scripture. See also the *Institutes* 4.14–19 (2:1276ff.), on worship. [Pages 179–181]

Please excuse me for explaining my action by letter and while absent from you instead of face to face, honored father. There are two reasons for this. In the first place, I feared that you would not be willing to listen to me on this subject, which is hateful to you and foreign in its aspect. The second reason is the great reverence I feel for you, which has not allowed me to bring any of these matters before you. Now, however, I judge that I should give you an explanation, either to bring about a reconciliation (to the extent that you are still offended at me), or at least to soften you somewhat until I have a better chance to satisfy you fully.

It grieves you that I do not follow what you consider the true way of worshiping God. If I did this out of contempt, as many people do, light-minded people who treat all religion as an up-and-down affair and who have no feeling in observing the worship of God, then I would not deserve forgiveness. But since I am driven by fear of God and the testimony of my conscience, I persuade myself that you will judge my action more tolerantly for this twofold reason.

To be brief, it cannot be denied that many crude abuses and corruptions exist in the church, hidden under the name of God. It is believed that good intentions will wash them all away. Meanwhile, those who live in such a way that they are sure they will win God's approval without the authority of God's will are (as the common saying is) drawing up their own bill without involving the host.

It should be established that God is to be worshiped in accordance with his decision, not ours. I admit that it would be intolerable for me to dare to make pronouncements on these matters out of my own feelings, as if I had better judgment than others, but it is not a question of who is wisest. It is a well-known precept, approved by general agreement, that God prefers obedience to any sacrifices. Therefore, not to belabor the point, God rejects anything that does not correspond to his will.

Witness to God's will must be sought from scripture alone, where it has been authenticated, and so I must guard myself against anything inconsistent with scripture unless I want to sin against God knowingly. It may seem absurd to you that I put in this category things that are regarded as sacred by common consent. I ask this one thing of you, though, father, that you not ascribe my judgment on these important matters to youthful frivolity, even though I am of an age often considered prone to accept anything. On the contrary, I began to feel this way when pursued and completely conquered by the testimony of truth, that testimony which is worthy and greater that any restriction placed upon it. Finally, I could not withstand what God's grace had granted me to receive by reading and listening.

Therefore, Father, when the sure knowledge that should guide my conscience makes me realize that something is evil, I judge that I should not take part in it, although I am distressed that I cannot abstain from such things without offending you. Nothing is more desirable or more consistent with my wishes than to obey you and win your approval. One thing holds me back (and I beg you not to blame me for this): If I should undertake anything against my conscience, I would be forced to act as judge against myself.

I hope my conduct is free from the blemish of arrogance and of thinking myself superior to anyone else. I cannot have what I want, since God has taught me what is right and wrong. All individuals will have to give an accounting of themselves before God, to show that their own ignorance was not a cause of harm for others, in God's judgment, and I do not see what excuse I could offer if I once turned aside from the knowledge of God and that worship of him which I am sure is the true worship.

I will not mention arguments here; it is not within my capacity, and I do not wish to add to your distress. But if you will allow me to touch on matters which are of the greatest importance and which are at issue, please hear what I have to say.

When I turn my eyes and thoughts away from that undeserved remission of sins which was gained for us by the death of Christ the Lord, and away from the sealing of that same grace which Christ himself taught us to show and apply in the sacred mystery of the Lord's Supper, and when I turn my eyes and thoughts toward that sacrificial rite and the application of the death of Christ which are effectual only through their own power, and toward that adoration of the element (even in silence I am pointing out which element this is), I must feel that the former are from heaven and the latter seem to have originated with men, to put it as inoffensively as possible. And when the question is one of worshiping God and maintaining his unleavened truth, other things are of no consequence. But perhaps you will accept these things less reluctantly if you take into account my ability and my poverty.

Finally, I ask this of you, Father: If you will deign to be inclined to hear me to the end, please do not regard it as burdensome to receive my uncle. I am sure that this will turn out well for you.

Farewell, honored Father. Please know that the one who has withdrawn from you for the sake of God is not unworthy of your kindness.

2. A Letter of Exhortation and Defense, Addressed to a Certain Pontiff

This letter, like a number of others in this collection, has to do with worship, and particularly with worship as reformed according to the Word of God. See "John Calvin, The Form of Church Prayers," in Bard Thompson, *Liturgies of the Western Church,* pp. 185–210. [Pages 181–184]

You do not know me by sight, but it does not seem unreasonable for me to cite your own free authorization as an excuse for the advice I am writing you. I hope this enables me to address you as directly as possible, without any roundabout excuses. For I have heard from you that you would willingly receive anything I might write you, and that it would not be a bother for you to read through it, think about it, and examine it. This has caused me to hope that if the seed of piety which I see in you is cultivated, the fruit will follow in its own good time.

This letter relates, therefore, to that cultivation. I would especially like you to consider within yourself that nothing is more fitting for a Christian than this: that he should not only censure obvious abuses and corruptions in the worship of God but also make an effort to avoid being rolled about in that filth himself by giving his consent to it too freely. Rather, he should learn that he must inquire for himself into the truth of God, so that he may safely rest in it.

I hope you will listen willingly to what I am going to add about our doctrine. I am going to be brief so that you may more easily see the road we are following and where it is taking us.

In the first place, many people cling to ignorance and superstition because they cannot even bring themselves to open their eyes to the light that is offered them. I consider you one of these, and I am showing it very openly so that I will not need to use a long exhortation to point it out and convince you. This one thing particularly makes a Christian man, that he determines to be on his guard against being deceived of his own free will when following a certain manner of worship. This is especially the case in a matter of such importance, where the salvation of his eternal soul is at stake.

We know that Christianity has been adulterated and corrupted not only by the idleness of the church's pastors but by ignorance, ambition, and avarice. I do not restrict this degeneration to the life and morals of the pastors. Several other things play a leading part in it: the transformation of the very truth of God into lies and deceits, the contamination of the worship of God with countless added superstitions, the extreme disturbance of church order, and the defiling of the sacraments. In short, there is a stunning disorderliness beyond all understanding. Few pay attention to this, and for this reason the *Regula Lesbia* is accepted as normal here to a great extent.

If the pure and natural institution of God is contrasted to the Catholic religion, there is the same agreement that there is between light and darkness. Each person, therefore, in an effort to understand and feel as he should about these matters, should not depend on the authority of a ruler or the precepts of custom or even his own feelings; he should consult the Word of the Lord and what it commands or forbids. The Lord did not speak in a corner; he wanted his will made accessible to the highest and the lowest. When you have persuaded yourself to lend a receptive ear to God as he speaks, and to yield to the things he has handed down to you by his Word, and to resolve to seek and receive the one path to salvation from him alone, then you will have prepared for yourself a wide entryway for learning those things each of us should grasp.

I come now to our doctrine. Many people condemn it out of prejudice, without hearing or exploring it. They are too occupied with some opinion or other that totally dulls the sharp edge of their minds. I am not going to mention the insults and even criminal acts that are imputed to us in an effort to keep everyone from tasting our doctrine. Only one thing can be charged against us, that we strive to call back to their own banner (namely, the Word of God) all those who are counted as belonging to Christ but who have been wandering about wretchedly. We are also bringing it about that all controversy over the worship of God is settled on the basis of his Word, so that each person may believe what is established as being from God.

What of our adversaries? They are making a counterfeit church, a sort of shield of Ajax, so that they may hide safely behind its empty facade. The prophets and apostles faced the same situation when they had to deal with men who were usurping, by their wicked beliefs, the very name of the church and its highest authority.

We acknowledge a church that rests on the sure foundation of prophetic and apostolic doctrine, whose single and unchanging head is and remains Christ. The church in which God's Word does not rule is adulterous. On this basis we conclude that the worship of God must be instituted in accordance with his command. Nothing handed down or introduced by men can be tolerated. It is for God alone to fix the law in our consciences. Only he has the right to ordain what he wants us to do.

This causes people to complain: "You have destroyed the statutes of holy mother church." We teach, following Isaiah and with Christ as our authority, that God is worshiped in vain when worshiped by the commands of men. James likewise says that there is one lawgiver, who is able to save and to destroy. Any embellishment added in the name of worshiping God will be found, on closer inspection, to be a pure fiction invented by the human brain.

If faith and prayer are at issue, scripture sends us to the grace of Christ alone and sets before our eyes our wretched condition, which brings with it certain damnation. With scripture as our guide, we are calling men back to the knowledge and preaching of the grace of Christ alone. The moment this is established, there will be a collapse of that absurd falsehood which says that merits are necessary for receiving eternal life.

This causes denunciations: "You are destroying the doctrine and pursuit of good works." Yes, of course. That accusation against us can stand, since every system of teaching about these matters in their assemblies vanishes away if compared to the earnest and accurate instruction in the holy life that our ministers transmit and inculcate. We take great pains to prevent anyone from deceiving himself by boasting of his works, and we openly teach that we can do nothing good without the guidance of God's Spirit. We have countless weaknesses, and nothing in us is strong of itself or of any consequence in proving our worthiness before God. The only foundation for that holy living which constitutes genuine righteousness is to cast everything else behind us and embrace the cross and death of Christ with both hands. To this foundation of faith we add true prayer, and we hold that we should direct our prayers to God alone, who calls us to himself. Knowledge of our own unworthiness should not keep us from running to the throne of grace with complete trust, through Christ alone, who is our mediator before the Father.

This produces weeping: "You have insulted the holy men and women of God! You have kept them from being worshiped and honored." Yes, indeed! We remember the holy men of God with sincere devotion, as the Lord teaches us to remember them, and we treat them with honor, but we cannot endure that saints should be transformed into idols or put in the place of God or Christ. We even dare to affirm that if those pious and fortunate souls are aware of the way in which the senseless world always concentrates on the creatures and unconcernedly disregards the Creator, then, I say, those souls are totally burning with zeal to call down God's judgment upon their own sacrilegious worshipers.

I cannot express how disgracefully the sacraments, whose practice and purpose are to confirm us in the fear and reverence of God and faith in his mercy, have all been overturned and falsified. And when we try to restore them to their purity, to their native condition, so to speak, we are accused of taking all the life out of them.

Our whole approach should be tested against the teaching of the Lord alone, and anything out of keeping with it should be condemned. Here the Mass is banished; there it rules. But the Lord's Supper has come back home to take its proper place again, that very Lord's Supper as it was instituted by the Lord himself once and for all, as even our adversaries cannot deny. As their only defense they put forward their own rite, and what they call their "received divine service." We rely on a better and stronger law, the command of God himself, which should stand inviolate to the end of the age. By doing so, as Paul says, we "show the Lord's death until he comes." No one can change anything in God's command without being guilty of rebellion before God.

I would be too wordy if I were to touch on other matters, so I will omit them. It is enough if what I have written has given you some taste which may lead you to a richer understanding when you receive a fuller treatment of the subject.

Farewell in the Lord. May he guide you with his Spirit, so that you may learn to respond to his will, and may he be willing to have regard for your salvation and peace.

Geneva.

3. For Bishops and Priests of the Papacy

The *CR* editors date this document November 1561 and identify its recipient as a possible Remond Chauvet. Calvin's appraisal of the office of the minister is definitively developed in the *Institutes* 4.1.1ff. (2:1011ff.) and 4.3.1–16 (2:1053ff.); his disdain for the papacy, its bishops and priests, in 4.2.1–12 (2:1041ff.). See also his Commentary on 1 Timothy 3:2–7, as well as Sermons 13 and 14 in *John Calvin's Sermons on the Ten Commandments,* trans. Benjamin W. Farley. [Pages 184–187]

Insofar as I have been asked what procedure ought to be followed in receiving as pastors those bishops and priests who might be converted by the grace of God to our side, I have decided to set down briefly in writing what seems proper, begging those who read this summary to excuse its brevity, inasmuch as it has taken me several hours to dictate it, since I am under the effects of a cold, which has made me heavy and slow.

Accordingly, if anyone, whether a bishop or a priest, who has been in charge of souls is moved by God to align himself to follow the pure doctrine of the gospel, but is unable because he lacks the knowledge and knowhow to teach it, then he will commit a rash error by attempting to do so. For the fruit of his conversion should lead him to withdraw [from his bishopric or parish], realizing what a grievous abuse it has been to carry a title without effect. At the same time, he should desist and relinquish his place to a successor who is deemed fit and who has been properly ordained. And he should be content to be received as a sheep in the flock.

But if a bishop or priest possesses the grace and knowledge to fulfill the office, and if he is willing to apply himself to that end, then he must first make a confession of his faith and affirm that he adheres to the pure and simple religion. Second, he must admit that his vocation up to this point has been a deception. Then he must ask to be approved anew and, in particular, must disavow what has been instituted by papal authority and renounce all those remaining unworthy offices which are contrary to the order that our Lord Jesus Christ has established in his church.

When this is done, I see no need to impose further barriers, provided he holds to his promise and faithfully fulfills his duty, joins the Company of the Ministers, who purely preach the Word of God, and submits himself to the discipline and order that they observe and keep. Meanwhile, his past ought to be buried and his sins forgiven, on condition that he is exhorted to comport himself in the future as one ought.

If one cites St. Paul's rule that elected bishops ought to be beyond reproach, I reply that, in my advice, the issue here does not involve a simple election but an approbation for restoring to integrity one whose office has been corrupted. For inasmuch as some have held the title of pastor to their condemnation, when the same persons promise to fulfill their office, which they previously clearly usurped, it can readily be accorded them by the church.

There are two imperfections in their status [however]. The

one is that they have not been inducted in an appropriate manner; the other is that they have been prevented from exercising their true commission. But neither is an impediment once they are prepared to reunite with the true church and are no longer held to be ordinary ministers but become newly confirmed in order to correct what had previously been defective.

It is important, however, to guard against ambition, and this in a twofold sense. One ought neither to break the order of the church for self-gratification nor to think that one can use the occasion for personal advantage. In fact, the word that St. Paul uses when he forbids doing anything out of ambition implies this hunger for conquest. Hence, the best way to resolve this problem is to do so in a way that avoids the quest for self-gain.

If those who profess to want to return to the right way feel hurt by these requirements, they are greatly mistaken. For it is impossible to accept them as Christian pastors if they have not renounced the papal priesthood in which they were ordained to sacrifice Jesus Christ, which is a blasphemy worthy of the highest detestation. In addition, they must solemnly promise to abstain henceforth from all superstitions and pollutions which are repugnant to the simplicity of the gospel. For how can they administer the Holy Supper unless they have been separated from the abominations of the Mass? Moreover, they cannot be ministers of baptism unless they have rejected the confusions by which it has been corrupted. In sum, the church cannot accept them as pastors if they do not feel obliged to do their duty.

All this presupposes, however, that a bishop is attempting, to the best of his ability, to purge the churches under his charge and supervision from all idolatries and errors, that he is demonstrating to all the priests in his diocese the way to take, and that he is trying to persuade them to give allegiance to the reformation to which the Word of God bids us and which conforms to the state and practice of the primitive church. That is to say, provided that he disavows those who do not wish to yield to the Word of God, and that he shows to the others, who are in agreement with the true servants of God, that he wants to establish and keep fraternal union with them.

As for temporal benefices, involving jurisdictions or revenues, although they constitute a corruption that is incompatible with the pure simplicity and spiritual government of the church, nevertheless, as long as things remain confused, one can, on the basis of tolerance, leave such benefices in their possession, provided one exhorts them to distribute the income to others, as being dedicated to God, in order both to keep them from profaning sacred things as well as to encourage them to live in a modesty befitting true bishops.

It would be better, however, if such people would willingly return their earthly lordships and jurisdictions and be content to be received as protectors of the church. Let them assist those who accept both the Word of God, as preached by the ministers, and the worship of God, maintained in its entirety. Let them do so without putting themselves in the rank of ministers. And let them essay to help as those exercising an oversight based on royal authority. And although imperfections remain, they can still act in a supporting role, being recognized as honorable members of the church in which they serve.

4. On Emigrating for the Cause of Religion

Calvin's high regard for marriage leads him to advise even one who has fled from persecution to remain faithful to one's spouse, though abandoned, as long as possible; nonetheless, he displays incredible leniency. See also his Commentary on 1 Corinthians 7:10–15. Compare also Paul Henry's comment in *The Life and Times of John Calvin*, pp. 470–471; and Carlos M. N. Eire, "Calvin and Nicodemism: A Reappraisal," *Sixteenth Century Journal* 10/1 (1979). [Pages 187–188]

If a man whose marriage has occurred under the tyranny of the papacy is constrained to withdraw from the papal church on the grounds that he is prevented from serving God as faithfully and purely as he ought, I would first of all advise him to win over his wife that she might be in accord with him. For since he is her head, it is right for him to lead her into the way of salvation insofar as he possibly can.

For this reason it is improper for a Christian man, under the guise of following the gospel, to abandon his wife. Rather let him strive by every means to draw her to our Lord Jesus in order that both of them might obey him with a common accord. Indeed let him do so not simply once, but let him continue to draw her, even though he might find her obstinate and rebellious. Let him do so unsparingly; and in making it his duty to teach and exhort her, let him ask God to touch her with his Spirit, for such is necessary, or all his labor will be in vain.

If one asks how long a husband ought to persevere in this manner, I cannot assign a period. I can only advise him to proceed as worthily and zealously as possible, so that day by day he might advance a little more and as much as God validates such effort.

Be that as it may, the husband must not become offended by the long wait or lose courage in the face of his wife's obstinacy, provided that he abstains from all idolatry. For in attempting to draw his wife to God he must not keep himself aloof or separate.

Furthermore, once he has done all he can, if he cannot live truly in peace without having to participate in papal pollutions, but is constrained to leave because of persecution, threats, or other factors, he is free to go, since he cannot be accused of not trying to lead out his wife.

Nevertheless, although his departure will not include her leaving with him, let him attempt, while being absent, to bring her out of the mire from which he has been delivered so that the two together may serve God. In doing so, no one will be able to reproach him if he later seeks a divorce or must separate himself from her. For where necessity imposes itself, there is no further obligation that he owes her that would justify him from turning aside from the service of God. Hence a man may leave behind such captivity when he has done everything he possibly can.

When a man with children is required to leave his country, whether willingly or by force or in order to flee idolatry, I would advise him to bring his children with him, as [they represent] the better treasure that God has given him. For if he leaves them, they will be immediately seized and held tightly in such captivity that he will regret for the rest of his life that he left them behind.

Moreover, his leaving will not protect them or their goods, unless he has freed them and divided their inheritance. But even this he ought not to do. For if he does, he will make them captives until they are twenty-five.

Further, even if their appointed tutor should be of the highest integrity, what could he dare attempt? And what authority would he have for selling or exchanging anything? And, provided the man is accountable, he may even have difficulty transferring annual revenues to the father.

In brief, whoever thus commits his goods under the name of his children is binding then with a rope or so enveloping them that they will be unable to extricate themselves from such an abyss, even if they should want to.

5. So That a Pious Man May Withdraw from the Superstitions of the Papacy

This letter appears to be written to someone recently converted from Catholicism to the Reformed faith. In particular, it answers a question about participation in the Lord's Supper. See the writings mentioned previously on the Lord's Supper, and see the *Institutes* 4.17.1–50 (2:1359ff.), "The Sacred Supper of Christ, and What It Brings to Us." See also 4.14.1–26 (2:1276ff.), "The Sacraments"; and 4.18.1–20 (2:1429ff.), "The Papal Mass, a Sacrilege by Which Christ's Supper Was Not Only Profaned but Annihilated." See Calvin's "Short Treatise on the Lord's Supper" (1541), in *Calvin: Theological Treatises,* trans. J. K. S. Reid, pp. 140–166; or "Short Treatise on the Supper of Our Lord," in *Tracts and Treatises,* trans. Henry Beveridge, vol. 2, pp. 163–198. See also Calvin's "Essay on the Lord's Supper" from *The Form of Prayers,* 1542 and 1545, in Appendix I below. [Pages 188–189]

I thank the Lord, dearest brother, that he has led you to a genuine awareness of his truth and has snatched you from those errors into which he sometimes allows his people to fall in order to humble them. Be careful to go forward in the simplicity of your faith, so that the Lord may strengthen you in it more and more. Now that you have become one with our Lord Jesus Christ from this world, and are a part of him (since he put on our flesh to enter into full brotherhood with us), you should undertake a life in accordance with the gospel's precepts. The sum of these precepts is that we should seek sure salvation in him alone, and should come at last to that life which is stored up for the faithful in heaven, in the hope and expectation of the resurrection to eternal glory. We should cling to the hope that our souls will live with him in heaven while our bodies are at rest in the earth.

You ask whether a Christian is permitted to take part in the Lord's Supper as it is celebrated where you are. The clear answer is "yes," provided that you are asking about Christ's Supper. When you examine the matter, you will find that there is no more agreement between the Lord's Supper and the papist Mass than between light and darkness. Men's wickedness and ignorance certainly cannot weaken anything ordained by the Lord, but I deny that the Mass can be ascribed to Christ as its originator. On the contrary, I say that it was devised by Satan himself to destroy the Holy Supper. Certainly it is diametrically opposed to the Lord's Supper when, under the name of a sacrificial rite, the power and effectiveness of the Lord's suffering are turned into a contrived act.

Open idolatry is part of the Mass too, not only when the bread is worshiped but when there are prayers for the dead, and when the merits and intercession of the saints are prayed for, and when many other things of that sort take place, which the Lord expressly condemns. The faithful are not allowed to share in that superstition any more than they were once allowed to sacrifice in Bethel. It is absolutely inconsistent with the confession of faith that the Lord requires of us.

This argument is treated rather fully in books published on the subject, and I ask that you read them carefully. Meanwhile I commend you to the Lord's grace, that he may instruct your will and open your eyes to let you distinguish black from white. Then I am sure you will be satisfied. You should free yourself from any pretense that you approve impiety in any way. May the Lord increase his gifts in you and show you what is right, and may he give you a resolute spirit so that you may recognize what is right and cling to it.

Geneva. June 15. Your Calvin.

6. Who Should Be Allowed to Take Part in Worship at the Roman Synagogue

This letter is dated June 21, 1558, and in the first sentence Calvin says that he has already made three hundred replies in the previous ten years to the question it addresses. His advice is that those of the Reformed faith should not worship with the papists. [Pages 189–192]

The questions you raise have caused problems from various quarters for almost ten years, and I have not been able to lay the matter to rest, even with three hundred replies. I am justifiably weary of it, and I judge that the best thing to do is to refer to my earlier writings so that people's insatiable curiosity does not consume my time needlessly. If I answer you briefly and concisely, therefore, I hope you will ascribe it not only to lack of time (by which I am indeed limited) but to a decision I reached some time ago. If people have such itchy ears that they long to entertain themselves with new answers every day, I will gladly allow them to look elsewhere. In the midst of so many responsibilities and nearly continual illness I do not have the free time to comply with everyone's wishes by writing publicly and privately.

Some people ask why it is not proper for us today to mingle our prayers with those of the papists, when we consider that the apostles could go to the Temple at the hour of prayer, and that even Paul could attend the solemn rite of sanctification.

First of all, we must understand that the prayers then current among the Jews were pure, formed in accordance with the precepts of the law. Even if the papists should adopt a pure form of prayer, in my opinion it would still not be right to go into a church with them. And yet [someone may say] it was not at all fitting for the apostles to join in the assembly of those who had crucified Christ.

My reply is this: An act that is pious and holy in itself is not corrupted by human wickedness. As I often say, if all the angels in the world were present at a mass, their holiness could not wash away its filth, and on the other hand, the presence of all the devils in the world could not make the Lord's Supper less sacred. As long as it is celebrated as instituted by Christ, it retains its own purity.

The apostles certainly did not go to the Temple at every hour of prayer, for they also held religious gatherings in private homes. But when they were offered the hope of building up the church, they used this opportunity. In short, they made an effort to frequent the Temple, not in order to be with their own race at public and daily prayers, but because it seemed likely that people who were inattentive in secular places would be more teachable and ready to accept the gospel's doctrine there, out of reverence for the Temple.

This is seen even more clearly in the case of Paul. He certainly was not driven by any religious feeling when he undertook a vow; he only did it to free himself from the unjustified suspicions burdening him, and to open for himself the door for spreading the gospel. He did not perform this ceremony of his own accord, or because he was asked by James to worship God in this way [Acts 21:23], but to bear witness to his weak brothers that he was not an apostate from the law of Moses. The apostles were free to enter the Temple and to bear witness to their piety by a holy offering, because they had no purpose other than to acknowledge that they worshiped the God of Israel.

Another question arises: If the shadows of the law were done away with by the coming of Christ, why did the apostles still follow them? This is easily answered if we understand that the Temple was the sacred home of heavenly doctrine as long as it stood, and that God was properly worshiped there. Christ ended rituals based on the Jewish law, but in repealing them he did not condemn them utterly as impious and defiled until he became known clearly through the gospel. You may argue that the light of the gospel was clear enough in the time of the apostles, but it is clear that Christ was still unknown to many and that others were illuminated by his rays but were remote from his full radiance.

This shows that there is a difference between ceremonies based on the Jewish law, on the one hand, and papal ceremonies on the other. The former were pure and holy in origin, while the latter were devised by Satan's artifice to extinguish the light of Christ, and were therefore sinful from the very beginning. We must understand the repealing of the law in precise terms: Christ's faithful servants did not need to desert their Temple and rituals (which were in themselves intermediary and neither good nor bad) before they had played their part in spreading the gospel.

Every time the apostles entered the Temple they did so out of concern for the weakness of the people, and wherever they went they usually attended the synagogues, not to pray (although they did pray there), but because there would be a crowd and people's minds would be better prepared for learning. In this way they would be more successful in teaching.

An objection is raised: If they did not pray in the Messiah's name, their prayers were misguided. I reply that the Fathers decreed that they did pray in the name of a Messiah, though an unknown Messiah. Certainly the effect of their prayers, which turned such great numbers to Christ so easily and readily, showed that the seed of piety was hidden in them. It is probable that the faith of Timothy's mother Eunice and of his grandmother Lois was praised by Paul [2 Tim. 1:5] before they had been imbued with the gospel, so that their conversion to Christ might be the fruit of that good root.

I do not concede that the shadows of the law were contrary to truth except insofar as they were wrongly mixed with superstitious elements and elements unconnected with Christ, or insofar as they were opposed to him. The Jews who sacrificed in their ancestral way before the light of the gospel was received were the companions of all pious people in a proper worship of God. This precept should remain fixed: People in earlier times were given the figurative language of the law until Christ began to shine upon them, and this took place gradually. Most people who had tasted the beginnings of the gospel sought their righteousness only from Christ and placed their hope of salvation in his sacrifice, but it is clear that they did not progress immediately to the point of freeing themselves from all doubt. This weakness was wrong and deserved censure, but Paul teaches [Rom. 14:1ff.] that it was to be tolerated for a time because they had not expected to derive anything from Christ, and it was a hard and bitter thing for them to abandon their long-established customs all at once.

On the subject of ceremonies based on the law, we must observe a sensible distinction between the sacrifices from which they sought expiation and those which had a broader use. Even today the religious observances which contain obvious and crude impiety are very different from those which are merely silly and trifling little things. Giving thanks formerly held a leading part in peace offerings and similar ceremonies.

Granted, the use of a figurative language was permissible when Christ was still unknown, and excusable when he was not clearly enough known. Nonetheless, it was wrong for the faithful who had been converted to Christ to make sacrifices to purify themselves or to engage in a eucharistic vow. (I am not speaking of bearing witness to one's piety, or acting particularly out of affection and to clear away a dangerous false accusation, as was the case with Paul in Jerusalem, at the urging of James.)

We must always remember that ceremonies are on different levels. On the one hand there are those which were pure at the beginning but which later, when the sun of truth came upon them, either became clouded and were finally abolished (as Christianity succeeded Judaism), or deteriorated into sinfulness by usage (as Judaism was used by the Jews in a superstitious and literal manner). On the other hand are the sheer superstitions that the devil devised to falsify the worship of God.

If anyone compares the law's purifying power with the lustral water of the papists, he is doing God a grave injury. God guided the people of earlier times in a useful way by that symbol, whereas the father of deceit has destroyed baptism with this foul ablution.

Farewell, best and dearest of brothers. Other writings compel me to break off this letter. May the Lord protect you all with his shadow, guide you with his Spirit, and support you with his virtue.

June 21, 1558.

PART III

Concerning the Worship of Images

1. A Refutation of Arguments Proposed in Favor of the Worship of Images

This letter is addressed to "M. de Beze." The *CR* editors identify the recipient as Mme. de Bèze. The letter bears the date of February 6. The editors propose 1562 as the most likely year. Compare Calvin's similar advice against the veneration of images in the *Institutes* 1.11.1–4, 8. See also Calvin's long and critical discussion of images in his Commentary on Exodus 20:4–6. [Pages 193–197]

Madame, since you are willing for me to respond to your report, I shall proceed by summarizing the arguments that are advanced by those who disagree with us.

They argue that the resolution to this question should be based on the exposition of the second commandment, which is correct, for it is the sole and unique ground of our dispute. Hence we must determine whether our exposition is in conformity with the truth or whether we ought to accept images.

They also admonish us not to take the commandments' prohibitions so literally, because St. Paul says, "The letter kills but the spirit gives life." I reply that their citation of this passage is improper. For in the apostle's passage "the letter" refers to the entire law, and the manner in which the Jews practiced this commandment shows that it was meant to be taken literally, as written.

Moreover, God had a reason for keeping the commandments brief, for he wanted his people to learn them. Nor did he want to obscure their truth, which is otherwise so clear.

Furthermore, they have cited this commandment against us, "Thou shalt not kill," in order to show that the commandments must be understood with exceptions in mind, seeing that it is lawful for magistrates to kill, as, for example, Phinehas did. I reply that whenever any exceptions have to be made in the commandments, they are made in deference to legislators, not to men in general. They cite against us the Manichean abuse in which the Manicheans claimed that it was unlawful to eat animals.

In order to prove their argument, however, they would have

to produce a passage that expressly commands the making of images and their adoration. Besides, there are numerous passages that approve of the executions which princes carried out in the name of justice in order to keep the public peace.

As for the Sabbath, I know that some want to see it as a ceremonial commandment. But I accept it as a safeguard for pure morals.

As for their reference to cherubim, I would reply with Tertullian in his treatise *On Idolatry,* in which he addresses certain Christian workers who saw nothing wrong with making images for pagans, saying: "Why then did Moses in the desert make the likeness of a serpent from brass?" My answer is that figures which were designed for some hidden purpose, not to set the law aside, but to be types, are in a separate category. That is to say, we must set aside those things which have been ordained for secret purposes. And if that seems to argue against our point, then let us hear what Tertullian writes next: "Otherwise, if we understand them to be against the law, are we not ascribing inconstancy to God?"

It has been said that one can interpret a commandment by considering what precedes and follows it. First of all it is said, "You shall not make for yourself any foreign gods," and finally, "You shall not worship them."

We must insist that the commandment is broken when our opponents worship and honor images, which they do when they attribute to them what ought to be offered to God alone.

Now sacrifices, consecrations of temples and the like, and incense are due God. But when you offer these to the images of the saints you are offering them to "foreign gods."

When I reflect on it, I find nothing that the Gentiles offered their idols that is not being offered to images. It has been argued that the ancients thought that their images were animated. I would respond that a few of the uncultivated among them held such a view, but the majority did not.

For example, we find in St. Augustine's passage on Psalm 113 a reference to the same excuses which people propose today. This clearly shows that no images existed in the church then and that people contented themselves with vessels only. Lactantius in his book on false religion says, "Why do you not address yourselves instead to him who is in heaven?" Arnobius says the same. "Sacrifice we owe only to God," says Augustine in *Against Faustus the Manichean,* book 20 [chapter 22]. As for incense, it represents only one aspect of sacrifice and was something unheard of during the time of Tertullian, who says: "We do not offer frankincense." The same is said of "crownings," which are conferred today according to the book *The Soldier's Crown.*

As for prostrations, I have held that there is a "religious" reverence that is owed to God and a "civil" that is owed to men. In fact, St. Augustine in his discussion of *dulia* says that there are two forms of worship: one that is owed to God and another that is civil and owed to princes. Now why would a "civil" bow require the same toward images? It is without order or reason.

I further maintain that there are things chanted in the church that are repugnant to God, such as [this one addressed] to the image of the Virgin: "Although not in everything, thou art everything." There is another verse that claims: "Rule according to your Mother's law." Are these not, I ask, genuine forms of impiety and idolatry?

Pagans attributed future events to idols, but the same are attributed to St. Anthony of Padua, to Our Lady of Good News, and to others.

It has been said that the law of nature does not prohibit images. But St. Paul says that those who worship them have exchanged "the glory of the incorruptible God" for "corruptible things." As for what occurred at Bethel, no image was erected, rather only a testimony that Jacob had seen the vision of God.

As for the "adoration" [of images], our opponents argue that they are offering only an "interior adoration," not an "exterior" one. But I argue, to the contrary, with Origen in his Eighth Homily on Exodus 20: "Restrain from both." He says the same in book I on Romans 1. Hence, I conclude that in accordance with the Word's true meaning we ought to interpret "to adore" in its proper sense and prohibit all honoring of images, whether "interior" or "exterior."

It has been said that anyone ignorant enough to worship images cannot help but say, "Images, I worship you!" Our opponents reply that they have given the image the name of that which is signified in the name they call it. Nevertheless, they continue to address the image. And that is why the people, being distracted by certain images, attach the saint to the image.

As for the cross, idolatry pertains to it when it has been consecrated—as it is the church's custom to do with wooden objects—when it is called "the cross of our hope." However, I acknowledge that the sign of the cross is very old in the church, and that the wooden cross falls somewhere between the sign and images. For this reason, the earliest usage of the cross was sound, but as time has elapsed it has become worse.

Nothing but the sign of the cross was practiced until the time of Constantine, who lived between the third and fourth centuries, and at the time it received no adoration. But when Helena found the cross [supposedly in Jerusalem] and sent it to Constantine, he set it up in the Forum. As for the nails, they say she threw one into the sea; from a second she made a bridle for Constantine's horse; and the third was set in Constantine's diadem—for which she was praised. We can only respond to this, however, in accordance with what the Word of God shows concerning that raised serpent which was shattered by Hezekiah when he saw that it led the people into idolatry.

As for Theodoret's *On Sacrifices,* I would hold that the sacrifices which God has ordained predate those of the Gentiles, but the devil has sought to substitute these lawful sacrifices of God with signs and imitations of his works.

The tenth chapter of Acts and the [nineteenth] of the Apocalypse prove that neither St. Peter nor the angel ever found worship [of themselves] good. Some argue that Cornelius was a Gentile. But, on the contrary, he is called "religious," and St. Peter went to him to lead him to the true Messiah. Cornelius was accepted by St. Peter not because he prostrated himself before him, for Peter had to rebuke him for that, but because what Cornelius said surpassed what was required.

Moreover, God's servants in scripture never received the praise that was accorded princes. St. Augustine in *Against Faustus the Manichean,* book 20, chapter 21, says the same. Similarly, the angel [in Revelation] says: "I am your fellow servant. Worship God." Hence, I conclude that if the prototype refuses to be worshiped, then even less ought we to worship images and other types.

As for the martyrs who have been interred under altars, St. Augustine says in the passage cited above: "We honor the martyrs by imitating them and having a share in their company." In chapter 16 of his book *On True Religion,* where he is addressing Christians instead of Gentiles, he says that the saints are honored for the sake of "imitation," not "worship." And of the angels he says: "We honor them by loving them, not by worshiping them." In his *On the Morals of the Catholic Church* Augustine says that in his time there were worshipers of images and pictures—both of whom he soundly condemns.

As for St. Basil, who teaches various things about the monastic life, I cannot think of anything he says that would contradict this.

Our opponents cite St. Paul and St. James on faith and works. But I will respond to this later in another context.

There exists today the same kind of ignorant idolatry as existed in ancient times. The Council of Nicaea [A.D. 787] cannot be accepted without leading faith into error. This council was called without the churches of Gaul and Germany being present. At the Council of Frankfurt the pope's ambassadors were present. We ourselves remove images. For Charlemagne, who prohibited their adoration, did not remove them, which resulted in our succumbing to idolatry. However, we do not reject all the councils, as we accept the first four.

As for our confession, which they maintain was derived by our ministers alone, everyone [present] contributed his advice and concurred to adopt the testimony of the Holy Scriptures. Other churches that have also separated from Rome and that are now dispersed maintain the same doctrine.

As for the Council [of Nicaea (787)] that reinstated images, I am unable to place any confidence in a council that denies its ecclesiastics the power [to vote their consciences], or one in which we are not guaranteed security, notwithstanding the ordinance of the Council of Constance, although it was made an appendix of the Council of Trent. Nor can I accept a council unless it proceeds in accordance with the authority of scripture and operates free of prescriptions.

We do not despise the church, nor have we separated ourselves from it. And if they should ask: "Where has the church been since the introduction of images?" I can reply: "Where was it during the time of Eli?" I think that our church has been in the hands of poor husbandmen indeed!

2. On the Lawfulness of Making Images to Represent God

The following document is Calvin's reply to a paper written by the inquisitor Matthew Horris (see Appendix II). Calvin refuses to accept Horris's interpretation of the supremacy of the gospel over law. He also rejects Horris's defense of images. See Calvin's discussion of the gospel-law tension in the *Institutes* 2.6.1 (1.340ff.); 2.9.3–5 (1:425ff.); 2.11.10 (1:459f.). Compare Carlos Eire, *War Against the Idols: The Reformation of Worship from Erasmus to Calvin.* [Pages 199–202]

The question is whether it is permissible to make images to represent God and to worship them by honoring what the figures represent.

In the first place it is undeniable that God expressly forbids such in his law when he says, "You shall not make for yourself graven images or any likenesses. You shall not worship them nor render them honor."

Brother Matthew Horris, in order to prove the contrary, alleges that we are not required to keep the law of Moses, that it is even null for Christians, and that those among us who willingly acknowledge its authority are "judaizers."

That such a response is both impious and repugnant to truth can be amply demonstrated. When Moses proclaimed the law he solemnly and rightly affirmed that it contains "life" and "death." Again, it is the "way," the "road" in itself. And even more notably, God gave the Ten Commandments as a perpetual and immutable rule of righteousness. For this reason he said: "Whoever does them shall find life in them." In accordance with this, our Lord Jesus did not say that we ought to put the law under our feet, but in expounding the law he wanted it kept and observed in its purity. And when he was asked what one must do in order to inherit eternal life, he replied: "If you would enter life, keep the commandments." And St. Paul, when addressing Christians, did not provide them with a new form for serving God; rather, he redirected them to the law, as in Romans 13, where he says, "Whoever loves his neighbor fulfills the law." For the commandments "You shall not commit adultery," "You shall not murder," and "You shall not steal" are comprised in the summary, "Love your neighbor as yourself." Again in Galatians 5: "Serve one another in love. For the entire law is fulfilled in this statement, 'Love your neighbor as yourself.' " Again in Ephesians 6: "Children, obey your fathers and mothers. For this is right, as it is written, 'Honor your father and your mother,' which is the first commandment with a promise."

In brief, the scriptures are full of such examples. And whoever denies that the law ought to be held in common by all believers, whether Christians or Jews, plainly renounces God and his righteousness. For the entire perfection of holiness is contained in the law.

Moreover, when scripture says that the law reigned until the coming of Jesus Christ, it is referring to the ceremonies. And this doctrine is so plain it has almost been turned into a proverb: "The moral law endures forever, but the ceremonial has been abolished."

Again, when scripture says that Christians have been set free from the bondage of the law, this bondage refers to the conditions and qualifications that were added to it, to the end that we might not be condemned by its rigor. Nevertheless, this doctrine does not rob it of its vigor. Thus, whoever wants to be obedient to God must conform his life to the law and submit to it. Hence we must conclude that Brother Matthew Horris, by banning the law of the Ten Commandments from the Christian church, blasphemes villainously against God, who is its author, and tramples his authority underfoot. For we ought to remember that St. James, desirous to show that it belongs to God to save and to condemn, reminds us that God gave his law for the purpose of governing our souls. It is true that the commandment concerning the Sabbath is in part ceremonial, but with respect to its substance and truth it retains its full force and remains valid for Christians to keep, although what pertains to its shadows and figures has ceased.

In fact, even this contradicts our hypocrite. For, with the exception of the keeping of the Sabbath, none of the other commandments contains anything about the ancient ceremonies, as St. Augustine himself attests in his *On the Spirit and the Letter.* Hence it follows that the prohibition against making images is contained in the moral law, and all those who willfully reject it reject the yoke of God.

Consequently, Brother Matthew Horris adds that the commandments of the law in their entirety are invalid among Christians unless they conform to natural reason.

To this I respond that if he means by reason that which belongs to the descendants of Adam, which has been corrupted by sin, then he quite decidedly deceives himself. For it is as if he were saying that we ought to base our judgments on the sight of the blind. I hold the opposite, that the second commandment of the law is both derived from and an extract of the order of nature, that is, that we ought not to represent God by any visible images. For God has not forbidden us to represent him on the ground of this commandment alone, but later on he provides the natural reason for which this ought not to be done, which is explained in Deuteronomy 4 and again in Isaiah 46: "To whom will you liken me?" For this reason all idols are nothing less than misrepresentations of nature that disguise the truth of God and exchange it for a lie. Similarly it is written, both in Jeremiah and Habakkuk, that images are nothing other than falsehoods.

As for what Brother Matthew Horris alleges concerning the appropriateness of displaying all those figures in which God has appeared, one would have to be a blockhead to grant him a single one of his arguments. For God never revealed himself in any visible form with the intention that one should later make displays of it.

Furthermore, in the visions that the holy fathers saw, God always provided unique impressions of his majesty that can never be expressed either by the hand of man or in objects of art. Consequently, anyone who tries to capture the majesty of God, as given in the visions, will falsify it.

Brother Matthew Horris's other argument is even more ridiculous. That is, that it is permissible to represent God by means of those things with which God compares himself. For in doing so one would fall back into unimaginable absurdities, for it would be necessary to represent God in the forms of mountains, lions, and gold. And it would be necessary to represent the judgment of our Lord Jesus in the form of a thief. Hence, everything this hypocrite cites only shows how repugnant idols are to reason and to the order of nature. In fact, St. Paul, in the sermon which he preached at Athens, which St. Luke records in Acts 17, does not refer to the law of Moses in order to prove that we ought not to represent God by visible images, but, addressing his point to pagans, calls their atten-

tion to the order of nature. Hence, so much the
people of God, we ought not to suppose God to b
silver or stone or anything else humans can imagi

As for what Brother Matthew alleges about che
marvel that he did not perceive the contradictory
own proposals. But that is how God dumbfounds
He admits that the Jews were forbidden to worship idols. Now,
in spite of himself, he must admit that cherubim existed only
during the time of the law. Hence it follows that they were not
made to represent God, as their form indicates. For insofar as
they were placed in the sanctuary to cover the mercy seat, they
signified that the majesty of God is invisible. And inasmuch as
they hid their faces with their wings, they admonish us of that
reverence and sobriety which we ought to possess when seeking
God, to which nothing could be more opposed than serving
him through the veneration of corporeal images.

He alleges that the reason why the Jews were forbidden to
worship images is that the Jews were inclined to idolatry, but
this explanation works against him. For idolatry is a general
vice for all people and is deeply rooted in human hearts. For
the source of idolatry lies in the fact that we are carnal and
apprehend God in accordance with our fantasy. Hence, contrary to his position, I conclude that insofar as the reason on
which the prohibition against images is founded is still valid
today, the same prohibition pertains to us and should apply to
every age until the end of the world. For until men are completely renewed, so long as objects are set before them, they
will find it impossible to resist idolatry. In fact, that is how
Lactantius, St. Augustine, and other Fathers have treated the
subject themselves.

Accordingly, Brother Matthew Horris ought to be ashamed
for claiming that throughout the New Testament we can find
no passages that condemn idols. For St. John in his canonical
epistle not only directs Christians away from idolatry, but he
commands them to keep away from idols. Further, although it
might have been permissible under the law to permit signs or
images owing to the people's rudeness, such has no place today
in the light of Jesus Christ's statement: "The hour is come
when the true servants of God will worship him in spirit and in
truth." And note the particulars of Christ's statement, for it
contains a stricter prohibition against outward images than was
ever required of the Jews. And when St. Paul condemns men

or having exchanged the truth of God for a lie, when they exchanged his glory for corruptible human likenesses and images of birds and beasts, he was not referring merely to the practice then but he was stating a universal rule—that we do harm to God in wanting to represent him in these ways.

PART IV

On Ecclesiastical Discipline

1. On Luxury

For an earlier translation of this document as well as an excellent introduction and extensive notes, see Ford Lewis Battles, "Against Luxury and License in Geneva: A Forgotten Fragment of Calvin," *Interpretation* 19 (April 1965): 182–202. Battles is convinced that "Calvin is here speaking of his arduous campaign in Geneva for the improvement of public and private morality. He is concerned with all forms of luxurious living and conspicuous consumption not only as economically bad and deleterious to the poor but as a threat to the very life of an independent Geneva, through the sapping of the moral fibre of her citizenry" (p. 183). See especially the *Institutes* 3.7.1–10 (1:689ff.), "The Sum of the Christian Life: The Denial of Ourselves."

The *CR* footnote says of this: "It seems to be an unfinished *lucubratio* [work undertaken late at night, by lamplight] of the youthful Calvin, to which his final hand was not applied in any systematic way. Incomplete phrases and the author's marginal notes occur throughout." [Pages 203–206]

I know how much ill will I am preparing for myself in the minds of those . . . etc. . . . . , since I am undertaking a war not just against one person or another but against this entire age. Perhaps some will thank me, however, and forgive the service when they follow my advice and begin to recover their senses. Others may look down on me from lofty places, as those lazy Maecenases do, or laugh at me with their usual jokes. No one endures criticism more indignantly or listens to it more reluctantly than those who cannot defend themselves by rational means.

It will be enough reward for me if some people return to a more virtuous life, and if I can expose the worthlessness of those on whom neither truth nor honor has any effect. I am sure that I can accomplish something for those who are sinning more because of the vice of the times than of their own vice; they are led by popular opinion, and they assume a person honorable if they see and have him as a model.* Now that truth has an advocate, perhaps it will take possession of those who are still teachable and only slightly corrupted.

The pleasures of food force people to eat when they are al-

---

*The Latin text is uncertain here.

ready full. If we want to name these monstrous luxuries, we must look for names that go beyond the natural. We admire and adore these amusements just as little boys fear ghosts in the dark, and to make ourselves boys a second time, we treat everything as if it were the dark.

Part of the remedy is to recognize one's own trouble. Vices often do not please even their own originators so much that they would dare to praise them. The pestilence has become serious indeed when men deceive themselves and seek defense for their own evils (Chrysostom, *Homily* 17, *On Genesis*, around the beginning).

They cite Joseph's coat of many colors and Rebecca's earrings and bracelets. How true is the saying of Cicero: "Many imitate the magnificence of Lucius Lucullus's villas, but who imitates his integrity?" In speaking of the coat of many colors, they show that their ostentation is boyish amusement. We do not condemn a proper taking of care, but we desire a moderation that is closer to abstinence than to luxury.

For a treatment of the first clothes, see Genesis, chapter 3. Our age has declined so much from those original standards of conduct that a chaste man or woman is now considered a monstrosity of nature. The voice of a dissolute man may be high-pitched and weak, but you should not think that his mind is continent because his voice is soft. Those effeminate and dissolute men are men in one respect, though, which it is shameful to name and which ought to make them justly ashamed. Maecenas would have received much praise for his mildness if he had not ruined it with licentiousness and luxuries. In the midst of all sorts of wantonness he restrained himself from shedding blood, acting violently against anyone, or using his power to suppress anyone. It is said that he was soft, not gentle. "All things are usually loathed when they are out of the ordinary and sordid" [Seneca, *Epistle* 20].

Some are so wicked and impudent that they will endure criticism if only people will look at them. They want everything so obvious that even people who see them while walking by will miss nothing. Do you think so many clothes are intended for only one body? You are wrong; they are "of months and days" (Seneca, *Epistle* 21). Excessive elegance is not a manly adornment. We are worse than children; inexpensive necklaces please them, but our foolishness is more expensive. There is never a vice without a patron. When we live to measure up to our models, we are not acting rationally but are led away from normal practice. When you have cultivated your appearance with great care, you should be ashamed to be outdone by many animals, and ashamed that there is nothing in your clothing to show frugality. (See Seneca, C. 1, *Epistle* 5.)

This ancient saying is truer than I would wish, that those who exert great effort in caring for the body are not much concerned about the cultivation of the soul. These people are not just weakened by soft living but are emasculated. It is ridiculous for them to want to be admired by the common people for their great expenditures on clothes, houses, and dinners when their stinginess, though cloaked, is so obvious. They are stingy toward everyone else in order to save enough to be liberal toward themselves, even lavish. Some dine frugally in order to build houses luxuriously; others withhold money from furnishing their houses and devote it to adorning their bodies.

We push one another into vices, and when we become, in turn, a source of evil to ourselves, we use custom and the example of the multitude as an excuse. Many people use the age as an excuse, or the place they live. "That is the way life is," they say. "What am I to do? Should I enter a conspiracy against public morals? Should I wage war on my country and my age?" I hear this and reply: Does a person die any the less from disease because he is in a city? Campania broke Hannibal, although he was undefeated in war.

I must speak about funeral services, and the way we extend our pleasures after death. What we cannot give to ourselves we give to an unfeeling corpse, as if we would get some pleasure from that.

It is a rare person who would not think, if you took away his clothing or hair, that his very limbs had been taken from him and that he was not the same person. It is the art of salesmen to conceal faults with excessive finery. The faults of individuals cause public error, and then public error causes the faults of individuals. The man who blushes at a cheap garment will boast about an expensive one.

The number of horses a man drives also relates to luxury. Cato was content with one. (See Seneca, *Epistle* 88.) Nevertheless, I will spare their ears. Individuals will not listen because they do not want to. I only hope I may be able to make them listen as a group. They would rather mix up all human and divine things and break all laws than to fail to serve the greatest luxury. We do not need to look far for examples. We have recently seen it in Geneva. If only poverty were consecrated in the churches and in public, so that afterward we would not be ashamed to accept it in private life! (See Seneca, fol. 211.)

Seneca, *On the Brevity of Life*, page 374, against caps, etc. In pressing this point contrary to custom, I will have charged God with a crime. If men lived life well, the manner of living ought to be sought from good men, but now, with public agreement on vices thrown in my face, we are boasting, in effect, that we have fallen into a time in which we cannot live a holy and honorable life amid corrupt people.

Against men's long flowing hair. It is Christ's glory. Do you dare put dyes on it? Is this not sacrilege? Perhaps this perversity of luxury led the anchorites in earlier times to prescribe a fixed standard of rather simple clothing for themselves, so that they might renounce the cupidity common to everyone. And then (as even well-constituted things slip into vice) the monks sought sanctity from hoods, caps, tunics, and trifles of this sort (or, certainly, they sought a reputation for sanctity). What would those anchorites do if they were living today? What antidote would they use to guard themselves, since they were unable to endure the luxury that was creeping into their comparatively uncorrupt age? Even with that antidote they did not take adequate precautions for the future. Many monks walk around so embellished that you might say they are working hard to make white clothing the means of achieving luxury.

No one should say, "I am not hurting anyone by my manner of dress, etc." They all bear the blood of the poor, for where do the more fortunate get their wealth except from the poor? etc. Especially those advocates, etc. The prophet said that your hands are full of blood. I say that the whole body is infected when it is clothed in such garments. They will say: "This is nothing new," and I acknowledge it. The human condition has never been so good that the better things have pleased the majority of people, although the luxury of the ancients could be called frugality when compared to this profligacy.

Remember the dire denunciation of the days of Noah.

You might say that certain people carry unguent shops around with them. The person who smells sweet all the time does not smell sweet.

Not only all parts of the body, but even their clothes are adulterous.

Our dinners serve our ambition, not our appetites. I must dispute Valerius's saying about Tubero's dinner: "Our ancestors wished to be magnificent in public but economical in private." If they had learned private frugality, they would not have been striving after public luxury. Now they carry into public the vices they conceived at home.

One can see many people who carry all their goods with them, like Bias. Others carry even more than they have.

The use of these adornments used to cause distress; now contempt allies itself with the increasing of luxury.

This talk of luxury-lovers . . . Oh, how long?

In neither case the clothing dealer whom, in Seneca (fol. 354), . . .

When you see our dances you might say that those cheerful men are out of their minds with laughter.

Seneca used "with an uncovered head" as a proverbial expression for anything which is without shame.

They should be warned to be more sympathetic to us, for they are given to vices that cannot be easily cured.

The greatest concern of some people is what they are going to eat, what they are going to drink, what they are going to wear.

A few things need to be said about the honest use of a mirror.

What used to be called womanly toiletries are now carried around by men, even by soldiers.

Our countrymen's hatred of children deserves criticism.

Augustine, *Epistle* 5. Actors live in luxury from your abundance, and the poor do not even have the necessities.

2. If Every Tolerable State of Discipline Will Be Refused

The matter at hand has to do with restricting admission to the Lord's Supper. Calvin steers between "excessive strictness" and "inexcusable permissiveness." Apparently a pastor has been accused of "excessive zeal" in trying to restrict admission; Calvin says that, if anything, the pastor had been too lenient and slow in attempting to exercise the discipline. See the *Institutes* 4.17.40 (2:1417ff.), "Of Unworthy Partaking of the Sacrament." [Pages 207–208]

Even if the lack of discipline that has caused your controversy had been tolerable until now, the situation has reached
such a state that, in my opinion, you cannot remain in a condition where there is no remedy for such serious evils. Because
you are uncertain about the degree of restraint you ought to use
in this perplexing matter, however, and because you want to
hear my opinion, I will give it.

If it is wrong to profane the sacred rites, then certainly any
slight obstacles that may occur will not suffice to excuse the
sacrilege. Therefore we need to define how far that profaning
extends.

We need not belabor a matter that is clear and obvious. I do
not doubt that the person who admits anyone he pleases to the
sacraments, with no selection or discrimination, is profaning
those sacraments. I admit that the church's practice has never
been pure enough to measure up altogether to the holiness of
the sacraments, and we know from experience how far our
ways fall short of the purity that is to be desired; but to prostitute the sacred treasures to everyone, however alien, is not the
same thing as opening them to the unworthy who cannot legitimately be denied access to them. The ancients were too austere
in this respect, and yet it is more than unbecoming for us to
have less reverence shown our sacred rites than we know was
shown in the past toward impure superstitions.

Unless we use some discrimination, therefore, to keep away
those who cannot be admitted without severe injury to God, I
take it as certain that baptism, as well as the Lord's Supper, is
being profaned. I do not see that we should admit a guarantor
who is estranged from the church, but it is unjust for the pious
to be deprived through the fault of the wicked. I know how
Augustine shrank from public excommunication. Although
drunkenness was holding sway everywhere in Africa at that
time, he expressed his opinion in a letter to Valerius that this
disease should be treated by flexible remedies rather than by
excommunication, which uproots and weakens the whole
church.

Nonetheless, we must always be careful not to foster sin by
relaxing the reins too much. I grant that excessive strictness
should be kept within bounds, but license should not be allowed. It is inexcusable permissiveness for there to be no law to
protect the sanctity of the Lord's Supper and baptism from
exposure to contempt and mockery.

As to your position that nothing should be attempted privately, I do not approve it when a pastor abdicates his office and deserts his station of his own free will, when his case has not yet been heard. A person with a sincere enthusiasm for building up the church will at least acknowledge that it is wrong of him to admit to Christ's Holy Supper those people who openly show themselves to be dogs and who, with no sense of shame, openly inflict mockery upon the sacred rites of God. Nor will this person be satisfied with the judgment of a few until he has recognized that the people are not willing to be subjected to a yoke. The question then follows: By what right is the servant of Christ held bound by those who openly reject the divinely prescribed order?

The delay is open to criticism, too, and we must frankly admit that this case has been taken up later than it should have been, and has not been defended vigorously and manfully enough. No charge can be brought except one of too much leniency, and this increases the guilt of all those who stubbornly get in the way; it does not lay a burden of ill will on Christ's servant who, by his slowness to act, shows that he has been too timid to take thought for the salvation of the people.

If I were in your place I would not choose to overturn the false accusations of excessive zeal and headlong behavior by any argument; I would only confess frankly that you saw from the beginning that the profaning of the sacraments was foul and shameful, but that you hoped for some correction when the people became more mature. You were tolerant because you preferred that they be shaped to obedience gradually rather than suddenly forced into order. While waiting for a better state of affairs, you have not kept silent about the difficulties besetting you. Now you are pressing on earnestly and vehemently because necessity compels you.

If you freely state this, and constantly press on with it in the future without stopping your efforts, then God will find a remedy for those incurable evils or will let you be sure in your own minds that, whatever others may say in criticism, you did nothing rashly. If you let this opportunity slip by, however, I am afraid you may afterward feel that you are held bound by some chain other than the chain of your sacred calling.

3. On Ceremonies and the Calling of Ministers

In this letter, written December 25, 1557, Calvin uses a principle of edification to ascertain the better action to adopt. See
the *Institutes* 1.14.3–4, 16 (1:162ff., 175); 3.20.33, 47 (2:896f.,
915f.), and 4.1.12 (2:1025f.), where he explains and applies the
principle of edification. [Pages 208–210]

With respect to ceremonies and above all the observance of
holy days [I offer the following]:

Although there are some who eagerly long to remain in conformity with such practices, I do not know how they can do so
without disregard for the edification of the church, nor [do I
know] how they can render an account to God for having advanced evil and impeded its solution. Moreover, all good and
faithful servants of God consider it a grave and serious matter
to submit themselves to things that are neither good nor useful.
Nevertheless, since we have to endure a number of imperfections when we are not able to correct them, I am of the opinion
that no brother ought to allow the above to be the cause of his
leaving his church, unless the majority support the opposite.
For in these matters it seems to me that as long as one has
sought, to the best of his ability, to procure what we know to be
the better, then he has acted responsibly. For even though what
some may wish to observe contains scandalous or impious consequences, nonetheless, if the latter of themselves contain
nothing that is repugnant to the Word of God, then one can
accept them. This is above all true when one sees that the majority of voices prevail, since as a member of the body, one is
not required to hold out any more or less than others do.

On the second matter, whether one must accept and approve
of as brothers those who have been improperly called, I do not
believe that it is appropriate to approve of their vocation as
legitimate. It appears to me that there are only two ways to
respond: one can tolerate their office; or they can acknowledge
their shortcomings and on that basis be received.

The first way can be justified on the grounds that today it is
not necessary, any more than it was in the past, to know if
those who accepted these brothers had a choice in the matter or

had to affirm someone else's choice. For this reason one can implore that if a prince forced the decision by his authority, his action no longer binds those who want an orderly method to be observed in the church for recommending and approving of actions for which they were not present, or were only called upon to witness.

The second way is actually better, of greater edification, and conforms more to the order of the church. It is that those who have entered the ministry in this way should quietly express sorrow for having been thrust forward without possessing a better foundation for their vocation. Moreover, it should be publicly declared that it is neither good nor useful nor reasonable to proceed henceforth in such a confusing way.

But I am astonished how in these interrogations no mention is ever made of doctrine. For it is interesting how we ask each brother if he needs to declare any shortcomings that require correction, while the principal shortcoming is omitted. More properly, they should say nothing until required to speak.

As for me, I shall conscientiously offer advice to any who equivocate about preaching on holy days, particularly if they find fault with the church but keep quiet about blasphemies that are delivered from the pulpit against election and the providence of God. For in doing so, in the midst of their examination, they allow the pure doctrine of the sacraments to be condemned.

This 25th of December, 1557.
John Calvin.

4. On Church Administration

See the *Institutes* 4.3.1–16 (2:1053ff.), "The Doctors and Ministers of the Church, Their Election and Office." [Pages 210–211]

When there is discussion of increasing the number of ministers, the decision on this matter concerns not only the consistory but the entire church. We must see whether they can easily be found, and whether the church's resources can sustain this increase in a proper way or not.

As to the qualifications of ministers and of elders (or rather, observers), it is true that no one, not even the best, can fill an office so perfectly that nothing better could be wished for. However, unless those are admitted who have been properly elected and who are outstanding in ability, there will be no end of upheavals and controversies in the church.

It clearly contradicts the order and basic rules of Christianity to believe that the wealthy, and those who are noteworthy for their position and name, should be chosen for church offices. In fact, we are true disciples of Christ most of all when we are not ashamed to subject ourselves to the administration of those in whose world there will be less reward and commendation.

The function of the consistory has its own boundaries and limits, and those who are called to carry out that function should confine themselves within these limits. It is their responsibility to watch over the Lord's flock, to be sure that God is worshiped purely, to admonish both privately and in public, and even to excommunicate when the situation demands it. When the consistory restrains itself and does not extend further than the Lord permits, there is no occasion for an outcry against it.

To establish some sort of ecclesiastical council (as they call it) in addition to the assembly that is held in the consistory is, in our view, inconsistent with the Lord's teaching. This new undertaking should be recognized and denounced, so that no window is opened for other changes in the future. It can produce certain disaster, especially because enemies of the truth will seize this chance for ridicule, as if on this pretext they might accomplish something against the state. We do not disapprove when learned and experienced men are chosen, out of necessity, to attend to the interests of the church, but this appointment should be temporary and unusual and by no means routine.

5. Concerning Church Ceremonies

This letter is dated April 5, 1558. The polemic is against non-sacramental ceremonies and against unacceptable additions to the sacraments. See the *Institutes* 4.15.19 (2:1319ff.), "Erroneous and Correct Baptismal Usage"; 4.17.43 (2:1420ff.), "On the Proper Celebration of the Lord's Supper"; and 4.19.1–37

(2:1448ff.), "The Five Other Ceremonies, Falsely Termed Sacraments; Although Commonly Considered Sacraments Hitherto, They Are Proved Not to Be Such, and Their Real Nature Is Shown." [Pages 211–213]

As a general rule, it is wisest to be content with a sparing and moderate use of ceremonies. The church has been burdened with such a mass of them that the brightness of the gospel has been almost buried.

In those rites which are called sacraments we must constantly be careful that the pure and genuine teaching of our heavenly master is not damaged by men's inventions. Especially when there is a free choice, nothing is better than to hold simply to the form prescribed by Christ and handed down to us.

If antiquity is used as an argument (and those who are overly addicted to custom and traditional ways of acting use antiquity boldly, as a shield to hide all their corruptions), it is easy to refute it. People of earlier times bore witness themselves, with heavy complaints, that they did not approve anything that had been devised by men's judgment. Augustine, especially to Januarius [*Epistle* 119], laments that the church even in those days was overwhelmed by a burdensome and intolerable slavery on account of unrestrained rites (although scarcely a tenth part of that labyrinth had then been constructed which now holds the world entangled in order to entrap souls).

Granted that many ceremonies were accepted long ago, quietly and tolerantly, we should hold to the distinction which Paul set forth, that the pure light of the gospel should not be obscured by legalistic figures of speech [Gal. 4:9; 5:2]. If no ground is yielded to the shadows of the law, how much less should figments of men's minds obtain this license?

If we properly and carefully examine what it is that stirs men to fabricate ceremonies, we find that they have all flowed from this source: each person dared to invent a new worship of God. God not only rejects all invented manners of worship but strongly abominates them. Obedience is of more value before him than any sacrifices [1 Sam. 15:22], and properly so, since his rule decreases as men make undue claims for themselves in this respect. It must be said, in fact, that as soon as men seek to worship God by their own judgment, whatever they produce is foul profanation.

To avoid wandering into a broad forest, I will come down to

a specific example. I have said that the proper usage of baptism and the sacred Lord's Supper is to be sought only in the teaching and command of Christ. The only begotten son of God wanted baptism to be carried out with water, but it has pleased men to add anointing with oil and exsufflation. If Christ's authority is holy and inviolable and receives the reverence it deserves, can anyone fail to see that baptism is defiled by these extraneous trifles? It has been so corrupted by these mockeries that it stains rather than cleanses those who mix these crude sacrileges with the washing.

I do not see the purpose of stirring a debate over mixing water and wine in the Lord's Supper. Christ uses the symbols of bread and wine to testify that his flesh was our food and his blood our drink [John 6:55; Matt. 26:26]. If there is a shortage of wine it is not at all unreasonable to dilute with water the little that is available, so that it may be enough for the whole church. If religion becomes involved (as if the mixing were necessary), this is not without superstition, for it means that the church is wrongly and needlessly bound by a new law contrary to Christ's command, and the rite is sought childishly, for no purpose. People want to mix water and wine because water and blood flowed together from the Lord's side [1 John 5:6], as if it were his intent to teach some such thing as this and not, rather, to give a token of a spiritual drink.

Cyprian's testimony should not be twisted this way either. He never argues that wine should be diluted in the Lord's Supper. Instead, contrary to those insane men, he asserts that wine should be drunk there in accordance with Christ's command. (There were some who kept wine away from the heavenly rite on a pretext of abstinence, since the people used it intemperately.) Since Cyprian teaches all through his treatise, therefore, that Christ's blood is represented in the Lord's Supper not by water but by wine, the things he says in passing about mixing them should not be taken as an argument for water. Besides, the ignorant misunderstand the word that he constantly uses for mixing; they always take it to mean dilute, whereas among the ancients and writers competent in the use of Latin it means to pour out of a container.

In another passage, wishing to exhort the pious to unity, Cyprian teaches that the sacred cup consists not of many drops of water but of many grapes, just as the mystic bread is made up of many grains [1 Cor. 10:17]. I do not deny that he speaks of mixing water and wine, but for a transitory purpose, because the wine stands for the blood of Christ and the water for the people. (If this subtle argument pleases anyone, he deserves to feed on the wind.) We should say goodbye to the inquisitiveness of man's nature, which has always run riot, and depend on the words of that one who is the sole authority for the Lord's Supper.

We see that Cyprian himself sends us away from himself and back to Christ when he forbids us to follow the custom of offering only water, and when he says that we should rather ask whom the Fathers followed, since others wish to imitate them. For as Cyprian says, if Christ alone is to be listened to, we ought not to pay attention to what someone before our time thought we ought to do; we should do what Christ did, for he is before all men. We ought to follow not the custom of man but the truth of God.

For temperate and receptive readers this will be a full and solid explanation of this situation. Men's wishes have been forced into their proper place, past custom (however old) has been put away, and the authority of Christ is preeminent.

Farewell. April 5, 1558.

6. To a Question About Certain Rites of the Church

This letter was written from Geneva on August 12, 1561. It touches briefly on several aspects of worship. Of interest is the interplay between what Calvin believed to be right and what he was able to lead others to do. See also Jean-Daniel Benoit, "Weihnachten in Genf im Jahre des Heils 1550." [Pages 213–214]

All of us recognize that it is extremely useful to add to the public confession some sort of promise that might rouse sinners to a hope of forgiveness and reconciliation. From the beginning I wanted to introduce this custom, but certain people feared that its novelty would give offense. I yielded too readily and the subject was dropped. As things are now, it would not be opportune to make the change here, because many people begin to stand up even before the confession has ended. This makes us all the more hopeful that your people will become accustomed to both while you are still open to change.

In administering the Lord's Supper I have sometimes used Paul's words, but I preferred to stop doing this because the words could not be repeated to each individual without a long delay; and if numbers of people went across during the recitation, scarcely one in ten understood what I wanted understood, and no one grasped the entire meaning.

We are very pleased that the Lord's Supper is being celebrated every month, provided that this more frequent observance does not produce carelessness. When a considerable part of the congregation stays away from Communion, the church somehow becomes fragmented. Nonetheless, we think it is better for a congregation to be invited [to take Communion] every month than only four times a year, as usually happens here.

When I first came here, the Lord's Supper was observed only three times a year, and seven whole months intervened between the observance at Pentecost and at the Birthday of Christ. A monthly observance pleased me, but I could not persuade the people, and it seemed better to bear with their weakness than to continue arguing stubbornly. I took care to have it recorded in the public records, however, that our way was wrong, so that correcting it might be easier for future generations.

Many weighty reasons force me to feel that the sick should not be denied access to the Lord's Supper. I see that this can lead to a headlong fall into many abuses which need to be countered sensibly and carefully, for unless there is a real communion there will be a wrongful turning away from Christ's sacred institution. Relatives, friends, and neighbors should gather, therefore, so that the elements may be distributed as Christ commanded. There should then be the canon, combined with an explanation of the mysterious sacrament, but there should be nothing different from the ordinary procedure of the church.

To carry the sacrament here and there indiscriminately is very dangerous. It is difficult to guard against a situation in which some people are led to seek the sacrament out of superstition, others from ambition, and others for empty show. The situation calls for judgment and discrimination. The sacrament should only be given to the sick whose lives are in great danger. It is preposterous for the bread to be brought from the church as if it were sacred, and for it to be carried in a procession is intolerable.

Farewell, distinguished men, brothers cherished from my heart. May the Lord protect you, guide you, and bless you forever.

Geneva. August 12, 1561.

7. On Baptism Administered Improperly

Calvin argues against the administration of baptism by lay people, saying that the Roman Catholic practice was based on a superstition and originated when "the need for salvation was attached to a symbol." However, he states that an instance of lay baptism that took place in an early, confused stage of the Reformation is forgivable and may be considered valid, as long as it is not used as an example for "a well-ordered church." He categorically rejects baptism by women. See the *Institutes* 4.15.20–22 (2:1321ff.). [Pages 214–215]

Your letter pleased us greatly, dearest brothers, because a place has been granted you in the city at last, and freedom of assembly has been given. God will increase this remarkable benefit with other, even greater ones. New and constant conflicts await you, and the fury of the devil will burst forth for a short time, perhaps, but you must press on vigorously.

We have not answered your earlier letter until now because there was no one to carry our reply safely. This is our opinion on the question put to us: No layperson can legitimately administer baptism, and you must oppose this evil severely; it is a clear profanation of baptism. This perverse custom originated in superstition when the need for salvation was attached to a symbol, and this twofold evil should therefore be nurtured all the less.

Augustine speaks uncertainly about this, saying that if a layperson performs a baptism when necessity compels it, this either is not a sin or is a venial sin. And yet the inviolable command of Christ ought to be of more weight: "Go, teach, baptize" [Matt. 28:19].

This knotty problem cannot be resolved without sacrilege. There is, in addition, the apostle's opinion: "And no man takes this honor unto himself except the one who is called of God" [Heb. 5:4]. We think, therefore, that a baptism performed by a layman is spurious; this temerity would not be tolerated in a properly established church. Because this has happened in your midst at an early stage, however, before the church's order was restored and when circumstances were still confused, the error should be forgiven and the baptism (of whatever sort it is) should be tolerated.

This baptism, performed improperly and only once, should not serve as an example. God condones many things in a fragmented church that it would be wrong to allow in a well-ordered church. In former times, when religion was corrupt, circumcision was undoubtedly involved in many faults and corruptions, but we have read that it was not revoked when the people were recalled to a pure worship. It is not necessary, therefore, or even useful to investigate all the circumstances anxiously; this would produce countless worries. What God forgave under the papacy we should also lay to rest.

We feel differently about baptism by women. Women went beyond the law of nature and forced themselves upon the office of baptism with monstrous audacity. We do not doubt that such shameful behavior should be strongly repudiated. Meanwhile, there is no danger that weak consciences are going to suffer damage, unless someone worries for no reason, out of excessive inquisitiveness. No one knows that he was baptized by a woman, and in the second place, an ancient decree of the Carthaginian Council prohibited women from the office of baptizing, so that the novelty of it (which would have been a fearful thing to men) will not shock anyone.

Farewell, best and purest brothers. May the Lord guide you with spiritual wisdom, sustain you with his virtue, and enrich you with all gifts. We pray for good health for the elders and for the whole church.

Geneva. November 13, 1561.

8. On the Disorderliness of Certain Ministers

In the case of two ministers who have taken up arms and called together their people for military action against opponents, Calvin urges that one be dismissed from the ministry, and the other suspended, for "military excesses." [Pages 215–217]

The love of God our Father and the grace of our Lord Jesus Christ be with you always, through the communion of the Holy Spirit.

Dearest brothers, we are greatly distressed at the report that the Word of God is being set forth among you in a disgraceful way, and that this is the fault of those who ought to be an example to others. We hear that the very men whose responsibility it is to encourage the people to peace and brotherly harmony have boiled over with the violence of strife and have called the people together to arms. How great and unworthy a misdeed this is! The news of it will cause a scandal that will spread everywhere, not only producing contempt for God's Word (since the scandal will surely be blamed on the ministers of the Word) but also giving Satan and his instruments an opportunity to overthrow and divide you so that the evil can scarcely be remedied.

Everyone sees the church of God today surrounded by enemies, but your reason tells you to maintain peace and harmony by all possible means. God's providence alone holds your enemies bound so that, when they mark you out for destruction at the slightest opportunity, you are saved from being carried headlong into that destruction. Therefore we must judge the same about ———— and ———— as about men possessed by evil spirits: once they have lost all consideration and rational thought about their ministry, their recklessness will bring final destruction on all the churches in your area.

We cannot approve the fact that ministers of the Word are resorting to bearing arms themselves, and to engaging in matters of that sort. We know that sometimes, out of necessity, individual ministers do not quite stay within the limits of their office. We know that dangers have intensified to such a point that each minister has to struggle against them with all his strength. And yet we cannot see how it is to be tolerated that ministers of the Word should go out as leaders of battle lines, and assemble the troops themselves and lead them. As a result, a minister becomes somewhat remote from his office and falls away from the high standard of his calling. This has happened particularly to those ministers among you; they have become hardened to soldierly ways, have put aside the character of a minister, and have burst forth into military excesses.

The situation compels us to speak, for we have been thrown into confusion by what we have heard. Both have acknowledged their wrongdoing, though one seems more guilty than the other, judging by your letter. Since you are waiting for our opinion, we have come together in the Lord to give you our answer.

First of all, such a great and unworthy crime cannot be covered up by dissembling and closing our eyes to it, unless we want everything turned upside down. If ———— is asked why he left the Assembly of Monsbelgardus, he will answer promptly that he left because everything was in confusion there, with no discipline. And yet if we prescribe discipline for others, should we not be bound by even tighter chains ourselves?

We see the trouble that is going to follow when a remedy is applied to this evil. The guilty parties will not accept censure, but will try to throw off the yoke. Nonetheless, whatever happens, we cannot allow the evil to be nurtured by our timidity. We are acting to preserve proper order and to suppress scandals. Many storms and tempests may threaten, but we must not relax our determination and our proper courage, especially when the reins should be drawn tight.

We cannot see that you can pass over what has happened there in silence without having the Lord's curse cling to you and hang over you forever. The passage in Paul (1 Tim. 5) that ———— thinks will protect him is no help to him at all. Since God's servants are especially liable to being subjected to false accusations, Paul wanted careful attention paid to their innocence. But ———— has already been convicted twice of attempted murder. The small cannon in ———— was blown up when, by a fortunate chance, the fire became visible.

———— has conducted himself among you in a way so out of accord with his office that it is amazing he could have been tolerated so long. We cannot approve his keeping a responsibility of which he has shown himself so unworthy. It is clear now that he must be disavowed, especially since he has aggravated his wrongdoing by refusing to accept your pious exhortation.

This is our advice on the way you should proceed: choose certain men from your assembly and let them tell ———'s brothers on behalf of the whole assembly that, after weighing the appropriate considerations maturely and properly, you have decided that ——— cannot be tolerated any longer in a ministry that he has carried out badly. Then ask that the church in that place dismiss him and give approval for another minister to be selected to take his place. They themselves would then acknowledge and approve the new minister.

If the church asks the reasons for this decision, it will be useful for you to tell them the things you told us, so that they may understand it better. But if the people of that place have been so seduced and snared by his arts that they will not agree with your advice and urging, then you must advise them earnestly to accept your advice. If they persist in their obstinacy, tell them that they are showing themselves to be schismatics, and that you will be forced to separate them from oneness with your body.

As to the other man, he is imprudent and impetuous rather than really wicked, and it seems enough to notify his church that he is being suspended from the ministry. In this way he may be humbled, and the damage done by the scandal may be repaired, and, when it seems right to them, he may be sought again and taken back into the ministry. They need to be warned expressly, however, that if they seek him again as their minister they must bury all memory of his guilt and not reproach him in any way for what has happened, that his temporary punishment should not keep him from being completely free to rebuke others as a minister should, and that his teaching should have the full force and authority that it deserves.

We would have preferred a milder sentence if it had been possible, but we feared that if we were lenient, the Lord would be less so.

Farewell, dearest brothers. May the Lord defend you with his protection, strengthen you with his spirit, and always increase his gifts in you.

Your John Calvin, in the Name of All.

9. When Disturbances Have Arisen Improperly in a Church Because of Scorn for an Experienced Minister

Calvin urges that a church unite in support of its pastor and not use minor questions about his election as a pretext for division and unrest in the congregation. He relies on a high view of ordination and election of a pastor to argue against casual changes of pastoral leadership. [Pages 218–220]

It distresses me greatly, dearest brothers, that, instead of having an occasion to congratulate you on the flourishing condition of your church, I must tell you how sorry I am over the sad news brought to me about you. The news of the death of our excellent brother ———— was bitter. In him the Lord had given you a very suitable and faithful pastor, which is an especially rare thing in these times when few people sincerely expend their efforts on the Lord's work. I am sure you have discovered how useful his work was and how honorably he conducted himself among you.

I hope that the man you have chosen will also perform faithful work, in keeping with the grace of God that has been given him, and that you will not be left abandoned. You should see to it, however, that others do not remain deprived either, as I hope you will do. I believe that those matters are being dealt with between you and those brothers by mutual agreement, and that their need calls upon your good faith for aid.

I am compelled to write you because of my distress of mind over your quarrels and strife, to which I see no end. I had thought that the quarrels were all laid to rest, and I thanked God for it, especially after our excellent brother ————, a qualified witness, had told me this was the case. It causes me the bitterness of a wound to hear that the evil which I had heard was dead is flourishing again.

In the past there has been discussion of certain qualities which you found lacking in our brother ————, but I felt that a satisfactory remedy had been applied, especially after he had submitted himself to censure. Now I hear that new strife has arisen, because some refuse to have him as their pastor unless he is ordered to give up his ministry and is subjected to a new election. I cannot fail to say that, in my opinion, those people are giving bad advice and are cutting everything down to the quick. This in no way makes for the building up of a church.

I do not understand how he was first ordained as pastor there and began to carry out his ministry. If the election had taken place in a proper way, there would be no occasion for controversy today. Granted that the circumstances were not without some defect, but perhaps you should consider that those who are there and who agree on the first ministry may be said to have elected him, in effect, even if there was no formal ceremony. This is especially true since there is someone in an outer region who is demanding that he be given the position and the opportunity to collect the Lord's flock.

It seems to me the height of ingratitude to reject him after the passage of so much time (especially when it is through his efforts that the church was built), or to fail to respect the man who opened up the way and the means for the church to be gathered together in the Lord through his ministry in the first place.

I acknowledge that church order ought to be kept fixed and unchanged once it has been established, but it is a very different situation when not even the most tenuous beginnings of a church are in place. What should we say about the many churches that have been built for the Lord throughout Germany? What about the men who exerted themselves to preach the gospel to them? Were they not accepted as true pastors, even without a ceremony? I do not think you are under the authority of men. I merely offer this as an example to confirm my contention that an election which is held when conditions are not yet settled need not be in the same form that should be followed when a church has already adopted its own form and order.

I cannot see any reason for your difficulties except that, in my judgment, pretexts are being summoned up from remote times. You should consider where you are sinking, if this [relationship] is broken once and for all. What decision will have to be made about the many baptisms, in the meantime? What about the serving of the Supper? I will add nothing more, since this is more than adequate to draw in the reins on those endless quarrels. If this does not satisfy those brothers who are zealous and too addicted to their own opinions, I ask them, in the Lord's name, to consider again and again the crisis into which they are leading the church. You are precariously situated. When it is recognized that you are so difficult in many matters, will your fretfulness not cause disgust and alienation of mind in those good and pious senators who received you so kindly? Will you not realize that we are all (in the person of that man who is the center of this debate) under attack by those who are striving for only one thing, to destroy all of you? It is amazing that you are not led by the example of the Guelphs and the Ghibellines, who could bring themselves to unite against a new enemy, especially since you have been called to a united profession of the truth of the gospel.

Those who oppose you on a certain point are beginning to rend you now, with a view to overthrowing you. That brother stands ready to repel them, and is sustaining the first attacks. How unworthy it is, then, for him to be harassed by you as well. The illness that confines him should be enough to soften even the hearts of those who were most angry at him, especially when you hear that a pestilence has been sent you by God, and that another pastor has already been taken. It is as if God is threatening to take away the pastorate which you will not allow to satisfy you.

I write you this to put out a fire that has been kindled. If there is still anyone who cannot agree, I ask you in the Lord's name to listen to proper advice and then to surrender to it peacefully, laying aside disturbance and strife. I hope my admonition will satisfy you. I have not wished to keep you from that final remedy, but I would much prefer that the trouble be corrected as soon as possible, without delay, so that all may come together in true harmony. If this happens, I assure you that you will be bringing great joy to your many brothers, who have your safety and tranquillity so much at heart that you will find them ready to make provision for it if needed.

Farewell, dearest brothers. May the Lord rule you by his Spirit with true wisdom, gentleness, and steadiness. My colleagues greet you cordially.

Geneva. December 22, 1551.

10. On Almost the Same Subject as the Preceding Letter

Again, Calvin urges that a church unite in support of its pastor and not divide over questions about his election. [Pages 220–223]

I wish I never had to write you about anything except to thank God for his gifts toward you and to urge you to continue your progress. Satan's wickedness has made me realize, however, that this subject has been snatched from me, for I hear that he has breathed upon you and that final ruin would have threatened the entire structure of the church if the Lord had not taken care of you and brought you help out of his great kindness. The evil was not long-lasting, but of what did it consist, and how is the fire to be put out when once it has been kindled?

Now that the flame has been extinguished by the Lord's grace and by the efforts of his faithful ministers, I have decided (out of fear that the same thing may happen to you again) to take precautions for the future by admonishing you and setting before your eyes the fault you have acknowledged. Please regard this as the duty of a good, fair-minded man, and if I seem harsher than the situation calls for, please do not refuse to accept my rebuke; otherwise your wrongdoing will be doubled.

I am confident that all of you who have to do with the Lord's flock will know who I am, and how I am led by concern for your salvation. I carry you in my bosom and heart as if you were my dear children. Ambition is not the reason for this. It is enough for me if you consider me your brother, and I cannot call myself a servant of Christ without acknowledging that I am your servant also. Therefore it is to your advantage that this admonition, which has your salvation as its purpose, should not be wasted or rendered useless by your contempt.

To begin with, I have never heard of such behavior as yours, when you say that you are pleased to have him address you and administer the Lord's Supper. A minister should be approved by the people before he is sent to undertake a ministry, but anyone who pushes himself in by another way after a church's order has been established has lost his proper calling. This does not mean that the people should be present when their pastor is chosen. Scripture tells us that pastors were ordained in towns and villages by the apostles with the consent of the people [Acts 14:24], but the passage makes it clear that the apostles presided over this ordaining with their own wisdom and authority so that, by their guidance of the people, everything took place properly and without disturbance.

The same policy has prevailed in the Christian church as long as order and discipline have had a place in it, and if you claim for yourselves the right to approve your pastors according to your own judgment, you are doing nothing but uprooting the order established by God for the honor of Christianity. There is another evil result as well: Those rash changes and constant innovations cannot fail to produce a definite danger and to make the church appear foolish in the worst way. This fault must be condemned.

I know that seeking this right would be natural because it would be gratifying, but it is much more prudent for that inborn craving to be stamped out once and for all. It gets constant use in human life and especially in the matter under discussion, for, because of Satan's craftiness, a sort of boredom with this pastor or that pastor seizes us between one day and the next, and finally the savor and taste of God's Word vanish from us. When we are carried away by fickle and unrestrained desire, we are no longer open to what is right and healthful.

Granted that you had some reason for your action and some "appearance," as they call it, it is still an unsound way of acting. What reason could there have been? When one of your ministers left to visit churches, another minister was put in his place with your agreement and approval. The original minister could not have been unknown to you; he had already attended meetings with you long before. Nor did you act out of conjecture about him. You knew what he was like, both in doctrine and in his manner of life. Anyone who despises him shows arrogance and pride against God.

What does it mean, therefore, when a man who has been properly elected, and who has faithfully discharged his duty as pastor among you, and who still has the gifts God gave him for that purpose, now begins to please you less? Whom would you prefer to him? Someone unknown? What chance do we have now of cleansing you of such obvious folly?

Perhaps you will reply: "But this other man speaks more

eloquently." Remember Paul's words: "The kingdom of God is not in word but in power" [1 Cor. 4:20]. Paul confirms this in another passage, saying that only the person who is "a new creature in Christ" should be of value to us [2 Cor. 5:17]. We should not depend too much on the flesh, and on that external appearance which dulls our eyes and may keep us from judging clearly, as we should. Beware of masks; that is to say, beware of anything that makes an outward show while hiding the fact that it is in disguise. We should strive for that which is excellent and true, and plant our feet on it. We must judge carefully when evil is not obvious.

I yield when the issue is recognizing someone as a brother, but when ordaining a pastor is at issue, quite a different investigation is required. I do not want anyone to be prejudiced by my words; a person who is unknown to us is not inferior for that reason in itself. I only condemn, as superficial and rash, our venturing to call to such a position and responsibility a person whom we have not investigated properly so that we could get a legitimate testimonial about him in advance. Scripture teaches that a pastor should be such a good man that he is recognized and perceived as good. If someone sends in his own name and pushes himself forward to be introduced among you, he has already branded himself with the mark of ambition and there is no need to investigate him further. I would rather have my hand cut off than to endure being brought in through such means, or to administer the Lord's Supper when I had been brought in. You have managed everything in this matter in a turbulent way.

One example will be of much help. The example of Moses relates to the duty of the true pastor when he expresses his wish that "all the Lord's people were prophets" [Num. 11:29]. We ought to recognize and, insofar as we can, yield the place to those who have received gifts from the Lord for building the church. I do not doubt that this pertains to our brother, as he openly shows, since he received that person even more readily than I would have received him.

We should examine the situation itself. Who first suggested to you that it was within the people's power for you to change your pastor rashly, as this one or that one happened to appeal to you more or less by his speech or eloquence? Who suggested that it was within the people's power to declare that it suited them for him to serve the Lord's Supper? Why not relegate this popularity-seeking to the cloisters of the monks? A different sort of restraint befits God's church. You venture too far if you immediately form an opinion on the basis of one speech.

The blame for this fault should not fall on everyone, in my opinion. I am convinced that one murmurer could have originated the disturbance. The Lord has humbled you, and you have been snatched away from that temptation, but I would certainly have opposed you more vigorously than our brother did. I praise his restraint, but I would have felt that I had to pull in the reins on that insolent disturbance with greater severity.

Circumstances make the trouble worse. You have a pastor who is held in prison. Is it excusable to arouse disturbances such as this in his absence? There is much tumult among people of other regions, but when you ought to be winning them over to you by showing moderation, you are causing them to consider you at fault, since you are conducting yourselves in such a headlong fashion in the administration of your church.

You need not be offended by my harsh words. If I were with you in person I would be criticizing that public misdeed even more vehemently. Perhaps I can weigh its importance and cause more accurately from a distance than you can discern them while caught up in the midst of the uproar and dust of the strife. I hope that you will accept what I have written in such a manner that I will be led to open my mouth and give thanks to God in your name.

If I have caused you sorrow I do not regret it, as long as (in Paul's words) your sorrow is "after a godly manner" [2 Cor. 7:8, 9], and as long as your regret for acknowledged guilt makes you act more sensibly in the future. You know that I want to console myself and, at the same time, offer you a cause for rejoicing; but when this evil arose our true friendship was revealed, in that we did not wink at your wrongdoing but have freely proved you wrong. No misplaced human affection has become involved. Anyone who complains about me should be sure that he has earnestly shaken himself free of his guilt, since censure is so hard for him to bear.

I am sustained by a far better hope for you than I have felt before. I am convinced that those of you who show yourselves obedient to God will also be open to instruction, and that you will accept, calmly and peacefully, the censures that are directed toward you in accordance with God's word, so that any bitterness that is in them may promote the soul's inner health and safety.

Farewell, dearest brothers. May the Lord foster you all in the fear of his name and in a love of truth, and give you constant increase in every good thing and in the grace of his Spirit, so that his name may be glorified in you more and more. Amen.

11. When Someone Has Been Removed from the Ministry for an Undisclosed Reason

Calvin writes that in a case of the disavowal of a minister it is required that public accusation be given and that a chance to rebut the charges be offered to the accused. [Pages 223–224]

We have heard about the disturbances that have troubled your church and about your subsequent change of pastor, and ——— has told us that he is not sure why you removed the pastor from his ministry. We thought it appropriate, therefore, to tell you our feelings about this briefly. We are sure you will accept this in the same spirit in which it is written. We are led by Christian zeal and sincerity and true brotherly love, and you in turn should receive what we say with that spirit of mildness which scripture especially recommends.

We do not need to debate at length whether disorder is threatening the church with imminent ruin, since things have reached such a point that a magistrate freely and on his own initiative removes or ordains ministers. Since the situation has been reduced to the point where strife and disturbances are boiling up and there is no place for ordinary remedies, it will be necessary in the future for you to learn from experience. Otherwise you will tear one another to pieces and cause the overthrow of order.

We do not need to write at length, since everyone knows the magnitude of the problem and realizes what may come of it. This is not the first time your church has brought this ruin on itself, and those who have caused the trouble are, therefore, all the less pardonable. We ask earnestly that you be alert in the future to guard yourself against Satan's wiles. He realizes that he is overwhelmed by the force and brightness of truth that the Lord has restored to the world, but he is, nonetheless, altogether determined to expose all the pious to reproach and disgrace by destroying the church's order.

This is our opinion on the disavowing of the minister: Our brother has told us in writing that he was not accused by anyone, but that the speaker's platform was denied him without any reason at all being given. This manner of acting is entirely alien to us. We have thought that we ought not to conceal from you what we have heard from him, because if there is anything wrong in your behavior we wish it corrected, so that his just cause for complaint may be removed, along with the scandal connected with it. However, we do not want our admonishment to produce prejudice among you; its only purpose is the discharge of our duty.

This is all we have to write about this matter, since it is not sufficiently clear to us. It is not that your integrity has come into question; we are simply afraid that we may be accused of being irresponsible if we go further when the matter has not been well explored. We do not want to urge you again to show us more fully what substance there is in it, but we would prefer that it be brought to light. This would immediately end all the harmful rumors. That is up to you. We will be satisfied with having urged you to take care that the church entrusted to you does not open the door to disunity and disharmony, and that the sacred order that should prevail is not destroyed by quarrels and disputes. You know that God's sons should be held in true moderation by a spirit of mildness.

We pray to God that he may guard you with his protection and take away and totally extinguish those quarrels which have had such power to divide you into factions, and that he may grant that you prosper in every good thing, and increase his gifts to you so that he may all the more be glorified in you.

Geneva. December 10.

12. Replies to Questions About Church Discipline

Calvin advises a church that people who request admission should be willing to make public profession of faith, and he approves the form of confession in use there as being in accord with scripture and orthodox faith. He says excommunication is to be used in moderation to remove scandalous behavior, restrain evil, and correct wrong action. See "The Catechism of the Church of Geneva," in *Calvin: Theological Treatises*, trans. J. K. S. Reid, pp. 83–139. [Pages 224–226]

Since Satan cannot altogether extinguish pure doctrine (which is a spirit, as it were), he is struggling to overthrow the church of Christ by this crafty stratagem: when discipline has been broken and loosened he cuts through the sinews of the body, so that the limbs become dislocated and a sad dismemberment follows. I wish that those who want to cast off the yoke and allow everyone unbridled license would realize that they are seeking the ruin and devastation of the church. They would certainly become eager for moderation and would subject themselves to the general discipline with a calm and mild spirit.

We do not propose to write at length about this, dearest brothers. We will answer your letter briefly. You ask our advice first about this: Should people who request admission to the church be compelled to profess their faith publicly? Secondly, you ask about the form of the confession accepted among you. Finally, you ask whether people should be excommunicated from the assembly of the faithful when they subvert order with their defiant behavior or their immoral way of living.

We do not see why it should be burdensome for a man to enlist firmly under Christ as his head if he wants to be counted a church member, and to do this he must expressly assent to sound religious belief and freely condemn the mistakes that corrupt the purity of religion. Abhorrence at these mistakes often depends on the circumstances of the times; as Satan devises new means of causing disturbances, we must oppose them with wisdom. We know that Paul commends to us "the unity of the Spirit in the bond of peace" [Eph. 4:3]. That solemn profession of faith is very necessary for fostering and preserving unanimity among believers. All who wish the church of God to stand unharmed will be glad that it is upheld by this support. We do not think there is any dispute over that general profession, but it will become cold and lifeless unless each person clearly renounces false and heretical dogma.

In the form of your confession we see nothing that is inconsistent with the sacred Word of God and orthodox faith, and we freely approve all the doctrine it contains. We would only wish that the letter to the Hebrews were not ascribed to Paul, since we are convinced by solid arguments that someone else was the author. But we do not want our vote on this matter to restrict the consciences of others, or for the church to be bound by a prejudgment, as it were, so that individuals are not free to make it known if anything keeps them from agreeing.

Although we may dislike the capriciousness of those who diverge from the general body of opinion because of trifling scruples, nonetheless, if someone cannot accept some rather difficult word or way of speaking (provided that he is in agreement with the real substance), perhaps it is better to put up with his weakness than to let the church be divided over some very slight matter. Meanwhile, we urge all the pious to be restrained and sober. Each person should draw near the others rather than, by his stubbornness, seem to be testing religion.

The safety of the church rests on nothing but the power of excommunication to cleanse it, to restrain evil desires, to remove shameful behavior, and to correct wrong ways of acting. Anyone who does not accept a moderate use of excommunication, especially when he has been admonished, shows that he is not of Christ's flock.

Farewell, excellent men, whom we cherish as brothers. May the Lord always be with you, guide you with his spirit, and by his virtue give you strength to complete the course of his holy calling.

Geneva. March 5.
John Calvin in the name of the brothers.

13. That Celibacy Should Not Be Required in a Minister

In this irenic and cordial letter, Calvin commends the discipline in the church and yet urges the group of churches not to use celibacy as a requirement for the ministry. [Pages 226–229]

Grace to you and peace from God our Father and the Lord Jesus, dear brother whom I deeply respect in the Lord.

When we have to write people with whom we have no

friendship or close relationship, we usually make excuses or ask pardon at the beginning, so that we will not be blamed for too much boldness or importunity. Although I am not known to you by face, I seem to have reason enough to venture to address you in my letter without making any excuse of this sort. Christ, whom we worship and confess in one Spirit, ought to be a strong enough bond of deep friendship. When —— told me of your singular goodwill toward me, I did not doubt that it was my duty to testify and declare, by all possible means, that I feel the same toward you.

It especially added to my confidence that he said you were delighted by my writings, and promised that it would not be unwelcome to you to receive private letters from me. I have complied, therefore, and all the more willingly because I judged that I was bound to you in more than the ordinary way because of the interest you have shown in me. I have nothing to write about at present except this one subject which —— requests, and which is easy for me to address. I trust what he has told me, because he studied with you for a year and can therefore have a complete sense of your feeling in this matter. Therefore, as I have said, since you have opened to me an easy approach to you, I shall not spend any more time in asking your pardon.

First of all, please be assured that I desire nothing more than to have a close friendship with you and to strengthen it by whatever services you would find pleasing. Our faithful brother here has told me so much about the gifts with which you are endowed that I readily count you among those to whom most is owed by all those who wish to be Christ's. There are not so many good men nowadays, and goodness should be valued all the more when it appears. I hear that you offer a fine example of wisdom and purity and holiness in that, although you are carrying out a dangerous and laborious responsibility there under difficult circumstances, you conduct yourself in such a way as to give complete satisfaction to all those who are faithful and courageous. Those who have the building up of the church at heart ought to respect your virtues and to embrace and honor you in the Lord.

As for myself, I wish I could show you more clearly how much I love and respect you. The one thing I can do is to promise you that my prayers to God will testify to that affection which you cannot experience through my human services.

Meanwhile, I congratulate your churches heartily, since the

Lord has given them pure doctrine and so many other outstanding good things. Not the least of these is that they have
such pastors to rule them and keep them in order and that they
are still endowed with good morals, an outstanding system of
organization, and the finest discipline. We can truly call discipline the best and, indeed, the only bond for maintaining obedience; we recognize its power, with great distress, when we
long for it and cannot obtain it.

This often makes me uncertain in my mind and keeps me
from carrying out my duty as vigorously as I should. I would
even be in despair if it did not occur to me that the building up
of the church is always God's work, and that he will cause it to
prosper by his own virtue even if all supports should fail us. It
is nonetheless a great and rare benefit to be aided by such an
indispensable defender, and I will consider our churches properly supported when they are bound together by your strength
of purpose.

I have only just looked at your confession of faith which has
recently been issued, and have not yet had the chance to go all
through it. It has the commendation of men whose judgment I
readily agree with. Nevertheless, I might wish that you were a
little more sparing in your approval of celibacy. (Please pardon
my naïveté, in that I do not hesitate to tell you freely what I do
not like.)

I see that your advice is not without a reasonable basis.
Those who are involved in marriage are less free for the Lord's
work, and it is expedient for those who want to consecrate
themselves altogether to the Lord to be free of this hindrance.
Then too, continence itself lends not a little dignity to the holy
ministry. Lastly, you do not use pressure or tyranny to force
celibacy upon those who hold ecclesiastical office, but you
counsel with them simply and convince them of what you
judge to be in the best interests of the church.

And yet, although I confess that marriage brings with it many
different impediments, and that it is desirable for the servants of
Christ to be free of these, nevertheless I do not concede that the
impediments are of a sort to call them away from their duty. I
would argue, on the contrary, that celibacy has its own disad-
vantages, and that these are considerable and not all of one type.
I am not speaking yet of the difficulty of sexual continence. I say
that celibate men are distracted by no slighter and fewer distrac-
tions than married men; certainly the difference is so small that

we might say that both are equally distracted. Even if it were agreed that nothing is more liberating than celibacy and nothing more impeding than marriage, it still should not keep us from taking thought for need. It is certain that many who are otherwise suited for the ministry cannot usefully do without marriage.

In the second place, I reply that the Lord has provided, best of all, the gifts that properly adorn his ministry, and we see that celibacy is not among them [1 Tim. 3:2; Titus 1:6]. I am glad that you do not command it by a definite law, but you must take care that you are not in effect establishing a law when you consider married men of less value, as if they have lost some adornment. There was no law requiring celibacy in the early church, but an absurd admiration for it became so strong that marriage was condemned as shameful for bishops. Afterward, the severity of a law gradually crept in and has produced countless forms of evils for us. What good it has brought I cannot judge. I always fear that it is dangerous for celibacy to be honored extravagantly, for good men may be frightened away from marriage, even when their need of it is urgent.

It seems to me that I have a basis, then, for wishing that any austerity which exists among you in this matter may be mitigated, not because it is an obstacle for you at present, but because it can be a great obstacle to future generations, for whom, as you know, we must take thought. If your reasons include some danger threatening you from the marriage of pastors, I wish the reason had been explained so that the danger might be avoided.

I am compelled again to ask indulgence for my countrified manner. I could not stop myself from expressing my fear about this briefly. Perhaps it is needless, but it nevertheless has some basis. And so that you will understand that I am not arguing a personal cause, I will say that I have never married, and I do not know if I ever will. If I do, it will be with the intent of being freer from many vexations and free for the Lord. I would not use lack of sexual continence as a reason for marrying; no one can charge me with that.

I wanted to offer you an occasion for taking thought about this. I am sure that you will see what is especially salutary and will do what seems best, after you have once applied your mind seriously to this matter, in accordance with your singular wisdom and long experience.

I am confident that you are administering this duty on which you have embarked in such a way as to need no exhortation. I would prefer to be advised by you, if an occasion should be given you, and if you should have the free time. Meanwhile, as I know you are doing of your own accord, I beg you to be eager to preserve unity. The times themselves teach us how necessary it is to unite in the Lord so that, with minds joined, we may fight against Satan and all his forces.

May the Lord Jesus preserve you, purest brother; I owe you honor in the Lord. I ask that you greet in my name all those who, in your opinion, will receive my greeting willingly.

14. On Certain Controversies Among the Pious Brothers

Calvin urges that it is proper for a church under persecution to assemble at night for worship and for marriage, burials, and baptism. [Pages 229–230]

The disaster to ———'s church troubles us greatly, but we must bear the situation patiently. God seems to be relaxing the reins on Satan and the wicked in order to try his people. In the meantime we should ask him to spare the weakness of his frail and tiny flock, in accordance with his kindness.

Those who think the church is suffering misfortune every time it is attacked by its enemies' madness or cruel violence do not yet grasp the rudiments of Christian warfare. As a result, this question has crept into the minds of many people and now occupies them: Should the faithful be allowed to hold night-time or secret gatherings? We see that a decision on this is being based on the outcome of the gatherings, which is a very backward way of proceeding. Recently, when they had held a gathering without any trouble, they thought that God was certainly pleased with their service, but now that persecution has arisen they are debating whether they are being punished for their rash behavior.

If this continues, even the confession of faith will soon be condemned because it inflames the fury of the wicked. According to those severe judges, it will be expedient to follow Christ only if the outcome is fortunate.

In this regard, Paul classed Ishmael's derision as the highest level of persecution [Gal. 4:29], because there is more danger from mockery and taunts than from armed cruelty. If the impious see us beset by adversity, they rejoice at our misery, and if our constancy gives way they hurt us worse with words than with the sword. We must remember what Paul said, that because we hope in a living God we must endure not only persecution but scorn. We should recall the example of Christ, whom Satan tried to wound with that virulent weapon: "He trusted in God that he should deliver him." We must not waver when we seem open to the violent desires of our enemies. If your brothers have been stunned or thrown into disorder by the first attack, it is up to you to support them so that they do not collapse altogether. You should even lift them, so that they may gather their courage again. They must not fail in their holy purpose, for this would give the impious a chance to rage.

If the question is judged on its own merits, the answer is easy. Private and secret gatherings, exactly similar to those now held under the papacy, were not considered wrong for the apostles. In those days, too, ill wishers were able to object and say that men and women could not gather at night and in secret without incurring suspicion. They were certainly burdened with many false accusations, and since military garrisons had quarters in Jerusalem, secret gatherings could even seem a threat to public peace. But this did not make them stop assembling. We see that they came together at a widow's home when Peter was captured [Acts 12:12]. There is no need to gather examples of this, for it is well known that this was their daily practice. History also bears witness that caves served as churches for the pious martyrs. It brought them much criticism in that they were suspected of theft and other crimes, but no matter what need constrained them, they nobly spurned the shameful deeds that they knew were commonly attributed to them.

Our brothers are armed now with the best defense of all: If the magistrates allow them to invoke God's name freely and openly, they are willing to come forth into the light of day and do nothing secretly. Because they are prevented from this by the tyranny of the magistrates, however, they are following the course that is farthest from civil disturbance.

We must feel the same way about marriages. Blessing them, as they call it in the papacy, is nothing but a pure profaning of them. Nevertheless, it is conducive to public order that a marriage cannot be called secret if a license has been obtained. We must not allow the holiness of marriage to be defiled and befouled by superstitions, however.

Nighttime burials are not forbidden by law in themselves, but it is useless for people to use this as an excuse to cover up their own pliancy when, at the funerals of their family members, they take part in and devote themselves to sacrilegious acts.

The same principle ought to prevail in the case of baptism. Even if imminent danger is threatening, it still is not permitted to do what God clearly disapproves. We know that baptism in the papacy has been corrupted by many base elements and almost adulterated. If fear were not a factor, all the pious would readily agree that it is wrong for parents to bring their infant children to a sinful baptism. It is superficial to seize upon danger as an excuse, as if the baptism itself could change its nature because of that. We know that bearing witness to piety is more precious before God than for piety to yield to threats and fears, at least when fear forces us to a pretense that is a tacit approval of impieties. We grieve with our pious brothers out of affection, but it is not up to us to free them from God's incontestable law. The Hebrew women in Egypt long ago did not hesitate to put their own lives at risk in order to save others' infants [Ex. 1:17]; it is shameful for parents to be so fearful that they defile the souls of their own babies, to the extent that they can.

I have written you this in accordance with the opinion of our company [of Pastors], noble and deeply honored sir. May the Lord always guide you with his Spirit, bless your holy labors, and keep you safe, along with the church entrusted to you. My fellow worshipers also greet you heartily.

Geneva.

PART V

Marriage Questions

1. On Questions of Marriage

Calvin offers advice on questions of marriage within family relationships and what constitutes incest; upon remarriage after divorce; and that a marriage vow spoken by one who disguises sexual impotence is null; and that child marriages and betrothals are invalid. See W. Fred Graham, *The Constructive Revolutionary: John Calvin and His Socio-Economic Impact.* Also see "Project d'ordonnance sur les mariages," *CR* 38/I:33–44, 105–114; Claude Marie Baldwin, "Marriage in Calvin's Sermons," in Robert V. Schnucker, ed., *Calviniana: Ideas and Influence of John Calvin*; and Cornelia Seeger, *Nullité de mariage, divorce et séparation de corps à Genève.* [Pages 231–233]

We know the degrees of blood relationship within which God's law does not permit marriage: a sister may not marry her brother; a niece may not marry her paternal or maternal uncle, nor may a great-niece marry her great-uncle; an aunt, whether on the mother's or father's side, may not marry her nephew or great-nephew. A first cousin, however, whether on the father's side or the mother's, is not forbidden to marry his cousin on the other side of the family.

It is not right to call into question anything in God's law as it applies to prohibitions, and marriages that are condemned by that law should be considered incestuous. It has become accepted by long usage, however, that first cousins should not marry, and the refusal to allow such marriages has become a cause for complaint among us. If anyone should ask for a final ruling on this, therefore, we will not simply reply that the man who marries his first cousin is committing a sin. This freedom exposes the gospel of Christ to much abuse, however, and we must remember Paul's admonition that our freedom should not become a stumbling block for someone else [1 Cor. 10:23], and that we should refrain from even permitted acts unless they are free of harm to others. We need not fear this bondage which binds the faithful together in a mutual pledge of affection, for consciences remain free in God's presence.

A similar principle governs the degrees of relationship by marriage. Some people debate (and even quarrel over) the right of an unmarried man to marry his dead wife's sister, and they seize on Moses' words as a pretext: "Neither shall you take a wife to her sister, to vex her, to uncover her nakedness, besides the other in her lifetime" [Lev. 18:18]. The same passage refutes their mistake, however, for Moses is condemning not so much the husband's incest as his insensitivity in wishing to take his wife's sister as a second wife. This represents an exception to polygamy. The Jews, in the hardness of their hearts, could have several wives at once, but God wanted to make this exception so that two sisters (or kinswomen, which is the same thing) should not be put in competition or rivalry.

II. Adultery has not been punished as severely as it should have been, and the lives of those who violate the marriage bond have been spared. It would be harsh, therefore, to prohibit a man from marrying during his whole lifetime if his wife has divorced him for adultery, or to prohibit a woman who has been repudiated by her husband, especially if they have difficulty with being sexually continent; one indulgence necessarily brings the other along with it. Nevertheless, it does not seem sensible, in judging the party who was at fault, to allow that person to fly off immediately to another marriage. The freedom to remarry should be put off for a time, whether for a definite period or until the innocent party has remarried.

III. Christ clearly excludes from marriage those men who are frigid, and eunuchs to whom manhood has been denied. Being misled is thoroughly inconsistent with giving one's consent, and the marriage vow of a woman who thought she was marrying a [real] man cannot be regarded as binding. This deception completely overturns the nature and purpose of marriage. What is marriage except the joining of a husband and a woman, and why was it instituted except to produce children and to be a remedy for sexual incontinence? A woman who has been deceived should certainly obtain a divorce when her case has been heard and well examined. There is no need to rescind the marriage, because it was null from the beginning. It is enough to state that a man who was not suited for marriage wrongfully and with wicked guile deceived a woman to whom he could not be a husband, and that therefore the contract which could not be kept by both parties was without effect and null.

IV. It has always been judged, and properly so, that marriage is not legitimate except between those who have reached puberty. When a boy marries, then, this is a childish game, and the sort of levity that deserves punishment.

First of all, it must be stated that those who are under the authority of their parents or tutors are not free or independent, especially in this matter. Even if the parents or tutors consent, or even if they are the principal instigators of the marriage— nonetheless, the contracts made before the proper age do not bind the children unless, after they reach puberty, they feel the same way, and voluntarily acknowledge that they consider their premature marriage valid.

If any parents betroth their children before they reach puberty, and pledge themselves and their possessions, they nevertheless cannot bind the children who are not yet ready for marriage. A contract of this sort is a profaning of marriage. If anyone has rashly put himself in a guilty position, let him bear the punishment he deserves. The terms of the marriage cannot be carried out, since the children, when they reach puberty, are free to retract whatever their parents wrongfully transacted on their behalf.

2. On the Appropriateness of a Man Marrying His Deceased Wife's Sister

This issue is assiduously discussed by Calvin at considerable length in his Commentary on Leviticus 18:16–18. It is of interest to note that Calvin chooses to remain silent on this matter in his presentation of marriage in the *Institutes*. [Pages 233–235]

On the question that is debated today, whether it is appropriate for a man to take in marriage his deceased wife's sister, it has seemed to us that anyone who does so becomes, as St. Paul says, an example of those who delight in pleasing men but who will never make good servants of Jesus Christ.

In the first place, we would prefer that those who affirm this abstain from misinterpreting the two passages they often cite, for in truth they so distort and corrupt them as to produce a contrary meaning. Moreover, the problem could be solved if they would willingly acquiesce in the presence of truth and reason, rather than handing the bridle over to an unrestrained appetite that only interjects confusion in the world.

Without a doubt, when scripture forbade the taking of a brother's wife, God was declaring that a marriage contract of that sort was a truly repugnant act and, consequently, incestuous. As for the diverse reasons they offer, they are worthless, seeing one ought rather to hold to what God propounds. For if the brother's shame is uncovered, then so also is the sister's [see Lev. 18:16].

Nonetheless, we can judge for ourselves that, as in cases involving murder and poisoning, so also in this instance of cohabitation, what God condemns is not the consequence but the evil itself. They argue that the brother's wife is not the same vessel [as when he married her] but has become sordid, so as to lose her chastity; they also insist on the same concerning mothers, daughters, aunts, and nieces.

But let us affirm the way God has disposed of this matter. For Moses addressed this problem, not in any subtle way, but with a simplicity that ought to suffice. There can be no doubt about what he wrote, or any shadow of subtlety of meaning. "You shall not marry your wife's sister, as long as your wife lives" [see Lev. 18:18].

If this were not the law—that a marriage with two sisters is illicit—then we could argue that such a marriage is acceptable. At least under the guise of this law we could argue that a marriage of this kind is prohibited only during the wife's lifetime, but that after her death it is permissible.

Now those who build their case on this exception miss the lawgiver's intention. For God is not concerned with turpitude or incest, but what he condemns is the cruelty of putting two sisters in contention with each other. Laws designed to protect humanity are abrogated when associated with laws defending incestuous marriages.

Certainly, God willed that the above exception be recognized in polygamous cases, so that if a Jew wronged his first wife by taking to bed a second, at least the fighting would not be among sisters. For this reason the rabbis concluded that God specifically denied his ancient people the right to infer this caveat from Leah and Rachel, as if the patriarch Jacob's actions justified it.

In truth, this law must not be restricted to blood sisters; rather it pertains to cousins and the entire parentage, for to despise any of them is to fight among one's own kin. If our interpretation is not accepted, then let us, following St. Paul's practice, shake the dust off against them for ignoring what is so plain to their conscience.

As for the civil law, when it is taken into account, it will nowhere be found that this custom was practiced or became a liberty under the Roman Empire. Nor will we respond to those who argue that we ought not to be afraid of an ensuing scandal. The only thing that hurts us is that those who maintain this view are so much under the sway of their passions as to dupe themselves into believing that Christianity cannot be preserved unless this lie is believed.

We readily acknowledge that when the papacy approved of this, it did so presupposing that God's law did not prohibit such marriages. But a right exposition of the matter exposes such an error and prevents us from continuing naïvely to hold it.

God wishes to grant his grace to all who refrain from involving themselves in frivolous curiosities and foolish love affairs. As for our part, we do not believe ourselves to have advanced anything of our own fantasies or opinions. Rather, we have striven to conform ourselves to the pure Word of God, which we trust any sensible person will recognize.

3. Whether a Man May Marry His Dead Brother's Widow

Calvin opposes marriage with the widow of one's brother, arguing from the law of Moses, setting aside the need to perpetuate the family name and appealing to the prohibition against incest. After addressing the matter in general terms, he urges "the illustrious Prince" to whom he is writing to obey the Word of God. [Pages 235–238]

It is clear what God has ordained about this in his law. Those interpreters are wrong who explain that a woman may not be taken from her former husband's marriage bed, or that if she has been divorced, she cannot make a valid marriage while her husband is still alive. It is improper to twist words into different meanings when they are stated in the same terms in a single passage. God forbids anyone to uncover the nakedness of his father's wife or his uncle's, or his son's, or his nephew's [Lev. 18:16], and it is absurd to make up a different meaning when he sets forth the same opinion about a brother's wife, in just so many words. If it is wrong to marry the wife of one's father, son, uncle, or nephew, we should feel the same about a brother's wife, about whom an entirely similar law has been decreed, with the same substance and tenor.

I know how these interpreters went astray. In one passage [Deut. 25:5] God commands that if a man should die without children, his surviving brother should receive his widow and beget seed from her for the dead man. They incorrectly and ignorantly limit this to actual brothers, although God is really designating other degrees of kinship as well. It is well known that in Hebrew all blood relationships are included in the word "brother." Even the ancient speakers of Latin designated first cousins this way.

The law we are discussing now, therefore, concerning marrying the wife of a dead brother, is only directed toward those relatives who are not otherwise prohibited from such a marriage. God did not intend to allow incestuous marriages (which he elsewhere condemns) in order to keep a brother's name from coming to an end. These two things are entirely consistent: for a brother to be prohibited from marrying his brother's widow, and at the same time for kinsmen to be obligated by the law of relationship to raise up seed for the dead, when the marriage is otherwise free from the restriction imposed by the law.

Under this principle Boaz married Ruth, who had earlier been married to his kinsman. History makes clear that the law applied to all kinsmen, but if anyone argues that brothers are included in this number, then by the same reasoning a daughter-in-law would have to be allowed to marry her father-in-law, and a nephew's wife her uncle, and even a stepmother her stepson. Even speaking of this is shameful.

Someone may raise the objection that the sons of Judah—Er and Onan and Shelah—were brothers and that nevertheless Tamar was married to two of them. The explanation is simple: Judah used this license wrongly, in accordance with the common and accepted custom of the nations. It is clear from histories of all periods that there were foul mixtures in marriages among oriental people, and that no attention was paid to a sense of shame. As often happens, Judah was led by evil custom to give to his second son the same woman who had been the wife of his oldest son. In condemning incest, God shows that this sin had run riot among the people. I consider it certain, therefore, that the law of Moses forbids marriage with the widow of one's brother.

Those who want to free present-day Christians from this law cite the passage [Gal. 5:1] in which Paul says that we must stand fast in the liberty to which we have been called and which has been obtained for us by Christ, but they ignorantly apply to the present situation something that Paul said with a very different purpose and plan. He was speaking of the observance of rituals that false teachers were using to enslave people's consciences by teaching that the rituals were necessary for the worship of God. There is nothing similar in the question before us now.

It is also easy to destroy their argument that we are not subject to the laws of the state. The law we are talking about must not simply be counted a law of the state, since it was taken from the common law of the nations and from the integrity of nature, as the words leading up to the passage show. Desire for incest had seized all the neighboring people, and God therefore, in commending chastity to his own people, says in his opening words, "I am Jehovah your God. Do not walk according to the customs of the land of Egypt and the region of Canaan." Then he adds the degrees of relationship by blood and marriage that prevent men and women from marrying.

Someone may argue that a law established particularly for the Israelites should not be considered a part of the law for Gentiles, especially since it is scorned among other peoples. I reply that the corrupt practice that prevailed everywhere in the Orient does not deserve to be called the law of the Gentiles, since it was the product of barbarism and the destroyer of chaste behavior and a sense of shame. No agreement or custom may destroy what is in accordance with nature.

We must insist, therefore, that the prohibition we are discussing is not one of those which can be repealed by circumstances of time or place. It flows from the very font of nature and is grounded in the general source of all laws, which is lasting and inviolate. God testifies that the custom prevailing among the Egyptians and profane nations displeases him. How can this be, except that the very sense of nature itself repudiates and scorns such foulness, although it may be approved by the judgment of men?

Long ago, when the Emperor Claudius married his own niece Agrippina, he avoided disapproval by having the senate pass a decree giving permission for such a marriage. No one was willing to follow his example except one freedman. That is a very different sort of case, I will admit, but I have cited it to show that the law of nature was incontrovertible among the heathen.

Fair-minded and moderate people may gather from this that we ought to maintain a great distinction between laws of the state and the law of nature. This distinction is inborn in human nature and fixed in the hearts of everyone. The solemn admonition by which God separates his own people from heathen nations, namely the Egyptians and Canaanites [Lev. 18:3], bears on this. In the land of Canaan, brothers married their sisters, indifferent to honor and respect, and the Egyptians were no better in terms of a sense of shame, as ancient writings make clear.

A law by which God is clearly drawing his people back from the impurities of the heathen ought not, therefore, to be considered a law of the state. To make the matter clearer, Paul sets forth the law of nature in a very minor matter: When he teaches that it is shameful and unbecoming for women to go into public places with their heads uncovered, he is telling us to take advice from nature as to whether it is proper for women to be in public with their hair cut short, and finally he concludes that nature does not allow it [1 Cor. 11:14]. If something is a part of the law of nature and cannot be changed, I do not see why it ought to be abolished on the pretext that it is a law of the state.

I come now to Roman laws that repudiate marriages of this sort. If these laws were founded on their usefulness to one particular people or the usage of a certain time or present need, or some other circumstances, then they might be repealed when circumstances change, or the keeping of the law might be waived in the case of certain persons of unusual privilege. The only thing considered in the passing of these laws, however, was the enduring integrity of nature, and not even a special dispensation is tolerable. Punishment may be waived, just as it is within the power of a prince to remit punishment, but no lawmaker can keep something from being morally wrong when nature declares it is wrong.

If someone objects that the New Testament does not prohibit such marriages, I reply that it does not forbid marriage between father and daughter or mother and son, either. Does this mean that blood relatives are allowed to marry? Paul's testimony easily destroys this objection. When criticizing a Corinthian who had defiled himself by marrying his stepmother, Paul says: "You tolerate a crime which is unheard of even among the heathen" [1 Cor. 5:1]. If someone objects that we are not talking about the marriage of a stepson and his stepmother, this argument is untimely; I am only using the example of the heathen to set before us an example of disgraceful behavior, so that at least we may be ashamed to see more propriety and moderation among them than we have. One of Paul's admonitions will suffice for me. Writing to the people of Philippi, he says: "Whatever things are true, whatever things are honest, whatever things are just, whatever things are of good report, if there is any virtue, if there is any praise, think on these things" [Phil. 4:8].

I have discussed the question in general terms and as a matter of argument. Now I shall address my words to the Illustrious Prince. I implore His Highness, and beseech him in holiness, to surrender himself and all his desires to the Word of God. I am persuaded that his desire arose from a worthy cause; perhaps the virtues of each party had produced a mutual love, or perhaps they were considering the public good. Nevertheless, the Illustrious Prince should restrain and moderate this desire, however good its origin may have been, so that he does not impinge upon someone else in following it. Paul reminds us that many things are allowed that nonetheless are not expedient. When a calm and orderly mind weighs everything, it will be clear that in this case the things that are inexpedient are also not permissible.

4. Concerning a Dispute in a Certain Marriage

Considering the times, Calvin's advice in the following letter is lenient and just. It grows out of Calvin's high esteem both for the estate of marriage and the sanctity of each partner's right to enter that estate, freely and solely on one's own. [Pages 238–239]

Dear Sirs and Brothers: Insofar as you have found it desirable to request our counsel and advice concerning the marriage vows between M. Jean Focard and Margueritte Heberarde—that is, whether their vows are valid—we, having assembled in the name of God, are in accord to offer the following.

Having reviewed the acts and proceedings that we extracted from your registrar, concerning what Margueritte said, her mother and sister tell us, quite flatly, that the girl was deceived and that they forced her into it. Her aunt—the widow of M. Pierre Focard—as well as his brother-in-law and servant, have also sworn that they knew of this all along.

Furthermore, there are three witnesses, of whom one, an Alexis Myot, solemnly swears that he was present when their vows were exchanged. A second, Simon Gaillard, says that when it came time for Margueritte to make her vows, he never heard her say the first word. The third, M. Pierre Nemauso, the royal notary, says that when it was Margueritte's turn to make her vows, he could tell by her countenance that what she was saying brought her no pleasure and, because he turned his back while she was crying, he heard her say none of the words one is accustomed to hearing. He also swears that, since that day, whenever he addresses her by her married name, she always replies that that is not her name, as he well knows. Moreover, he has sworn under oath that he did not want to record this marriage, which he witnessed, since he knew that it was not of God, insofar as Margueritte had not consented to it.

Hence we note that although a ceremony for the exchanging of marriage vows occurred, not a single witness swears that the girl said anything by way of consent. The second witness says that he is uncertain that she said anything. The third—whose testimony we can most trust, since he is a notary public and accountable for recording marriages—swears he saw signs of disagreement.

Now, inasmuch as the girl cannot be expected to settle this matter, it remains to know who can. The notary public's testimony is amply sufficient. The aunt, the brother-in-law, and Pierre Havart's sister also constitute a valid witness. Above all, there is the mother's confession that she forced her daughter into it. Hence we conclude that the girl was forced into it; consequently, no foundation for marriage exists. Furthermore, M. Jean Focard himself affirms that he has not had an opportunity to speak to Margueritte for some time and that he has never understood what she actually said at their wedding. Therefore, given the present facts, we cannot rule that a marriage occurred. Rather, since the act took place contrary to order and reason, we judge it to be null.

Nevertheless, since this is a delicate matter and could cause a great deal of conflict between the parties, and, in order to forestall any unfortunate repercussions as well as to prevent future rumors and reproach, we are of the opinion that M. Focard should summon the mother and the girl before the common court and there have the marriage annulled. The two should solemnly swear and confirm what they have attested to be true. In any event, in our definitive judgment, their marriage vows are null, and each party is free to marry someone else.

5. Concerning a Pious Woman Treated Harshly by Her Husband Because of Her Religion

In this instance, Calvin is more circumspect. He urges faithfulness to one's spouse, almost to the breaking point. Compare Calvin's advice in his Commentaries on 1 Corinthians 7:13 and 1 Peter 3:1. In these cases, Calvin's plea is evangelical, that one might "lure" one's spouse to the faith. [Pages 239–241]

At issue is a request from a pious woman who, because of her desire to follow the truth and pure religion, has been treated badly by her husband and subjected to cruel and harsh servitude. Thus she wishes to know if it is permissible to leave her husband and to come here or withdraw to another church where she might rest her conscience in peace. Accordingly, we offer the following advice.

First of all, with respect to her perplexity and agony, we are filled with pity and compassion for her and are drawn to pray that it will please God to give her such a sense of relief that she will be able to find the wherewithal to rejoice in him. Nevertheless, since she has asked for our counsel regarding what is permissible, our duty is to respond, purely and simply, on the basis of what God reveals to us in his Word, closing our eyes to all else. For this reason, we beg her not to take offense if our advice does not correspond with her hope. For it is necessary that she and we follow what the Master has ordained, without mingling our desires with it.

Now, with regard to the bond of marriage, one must remember that a believing party cannot, of his or her free will, divorce the unbeliever, as St. Paul makes clear in 1 Corinthians 7:13. Without a doubt, St. Paul emphasizes this, fully knowing the suffering each party may be experiencing. For at that time the pagans and the Jews were no less poisoned against the Christian religion than the papists are today. But St. Paul commands the believing partner, who continues to persevere in the truth of God, not to leave the partner who resists God.

In brief, we ought so to prefer God and Jesus Christ to the whole world that fathers, children, husbands, and wives cease to constitute something we value. So much is this so, that if we cannot adhere to him and renounce all else, we ought to make ourselves do so. This does not mean that Christianity ought to abrogate the order of nature. Where the two parties consent, it is especially fitting for the Christian wife to double her efforts to be submissive to her husband—here regarded as an enemy of the truth—in order to win him if at all possible, as St. Peter advises in 1 Peter 3:1.

Nevertheless, as matters stand today in the papal church, a believing wife ought not to relinquish her hope without striving and trying to direct her husband toward the road of salvation. No matter how great his obstinacy might be, she must not let herself be diverted from the faith; rather she must affirm it with constancy and steadfastness—whatever the dangers might be.

However, if the above party should be persecuted to the extent that she is in danger of denying her hope, then she is justified in fleeing. When a wife (or husband, as the case may be) has made her confession of faith and demonstrated how necessary it is not to consent to the abominations of the papacy, and if persecution arises against her for having done so and she is in grave peril, she may justly flee when God grants her an occasion to escape. For that does not constitute a willful divorce but occurs because of persecution.

Hence it is appropriate that the good lady who has sought our counsel endure until the above occurs. For according to her letters, she currently only holds her peace and quietly goes along; being required to taint herself before idols, she bows before them in condescension. For this reason she may not justify leaving her husband until she has amply declared her faith and resisted greater pressures than presently encountered. Therefore she needs to pray for God to strengthen her, then she needs to fight more valiantly than she has, drawing upon the power of the Holy Spirit, to show her husband her faith, doing so in gentleness and humility, explaining to him that she must not offend God for the sake of pleasing him.

We have also taken into consideration her husband's rudeness and cruelty, of which she has advised us. But that ought not to prevent her from taking heart to commend the matter to God. For whenever we are so preoccupied with fear that we are afraid to do what we ought, then we are guilty of infidelity. That is the foundation on which we should build.

If, after having attempted what we have advised, she should come into imminent peril, or her husband should persecute her to the point of death, then she is free to exercise that liberty which our Lord grants to all his own, i.e., to flee ravenous wolves.

July 22, 1552.

6. If One Party in a Marriage Should Contract Elephantiasis

In this letter Calvin considers the very perplexing situation in which a husband contracts a disease that intensifies sexual craving while rendering him contagious. He urges restraint on the part of the sick man and says that his wife, pending a judicial action, should be allowed "to live as a widow," while attending her husband. [Pages 241–242]

We hope that our last letter reached you before yours was delivered to us. The subject you are asking about is very perplexing. Disease is not a proper cause for divorce, no matter what it is, and one party in a marriage remains bound to the other as long as the marriage remains firm. Paul urges both parties to give the goodwill that is owed by the husband to the wife and by the wife to the husband [1 Cor. 7:3].

We consider that the marriage bond is indissoluble, even if the wife is separated from the marriage bed. The question arises, however: If the husband contracts elephantiasis (which is commonly called leprosy), does this free the woman from her marital obligation? They say that men with elephantiasis may suffer from sexual craving and be unusually full of sexual desire, and the husband will use this as an excuse to say that he needs his wife.

If a man with elephantiasis has any sense of humanity, however, he will first refrain from injuring his wife and children and then take thought for the human race, to keep the contagion from creeping about more widely. He is caught in a situation where he cannot perform his duty as a husband or father and is even, in a certain way, an enemy of the public welfare. Unless he is overcome by a brutish sort of stupor, he should realize that he is loathsome to everyone and should hide himself away out of a sense of self-restraint.

We do not want to be cruel, and we do not venture to obligate the woman to share a home and marriage bed with a husband who is forgetful of all the laws of nature. We feel that she must be allowed to live as a widow, after a legal investigation by judges has intervened. Meanwhile, she should continue to attend her husband and perform any duties she can, provided that he does not require of her anything virtually unnatural.

Farewell, best and purest of brothers. May the Lord always be with you, protect you, and guide you with his Spirit.

Geneva. December 2, 1561.

7. On a Marriage That Was Improperly Instituted

Calvin responds to a question about a couple married clandestinely who refused to have their marriage confirmed. In fact the wife has separated herself so that it has become a question of voluntary divorce, and the husband has taken another wife. Calvin argues that the original pledge is binding. This letter, with the others on marriage, shows Calvin's sense of pastoral discipline, his reserve in making judgments as an outsider, and his commonsense approach to legal and moral questions. [Pages 242–244]

So many people ask my advice that I am not always free to comply with all their requests, but I am not so capricious as to be displeased by their pious concerns. My excuse for not answering your letter is a very truthful one: I had only glanced at it casually and hastily, and had planned to read it again more carefully, but (and this is something that happens to me very rarely, or never) I lost it. Therefore I thought it would be rash for me to answer it until I understood better what you were asking and what knotty problems you wanted me to solve.

All good men properly disapprove of clandestine marriages, which offer an opportunity and even, in fact, an open door to many disgraceful acts. Also, I wish the man (whoever he is) had married someone other than his own first cousin. This sort of marriage between cousins has always been permitted by the law of Moses as well as the general law of nations, but we must remember what Paul said, that the faithful should not allow themselves to do more than is expedient [1 Cor. 6:12]. We have not allowed that degree of relationship in marriages among us, in order that the gospel of Christ might not be exposed to abuse.

The people you have written about are indulging their fleshly desires too much, and prefer to undergo the disgrace of being thought promiscuous rather than to acknowledge their marriage. If they must choose between evils, it is better for them to buy back their freedom with money than to submerge themselves into this labyrinth. As soon as the woman grew tired of her husband, she ignored her pledged faith and made a divorce, and the husband, in the same casual way, flew off to a new marriage with no legal action taken. They both deserve severe punishment, and neither deserves that you should investigate this perplexed matter so carefully on their behalf.

What solution can be found? By shaking off her husband's yoke, the wife has violated her pledge of faith. This voluntary divorce is close to the appearance of adultery, whether it was prompted by capriciousness or sexual desire. If the situation remains unresolved after he has tried reconciliation often and with no effect, the husband should submit to arbitration to force her to carry out her duty. This is to be preferred to breaking the sacred and indissoluble bond and taking the decision-making on himself.

For him to take a second wife is nothing but pure adultery veiled by the honorable title of marriage. His wife's departure did not set him free until it is legally determined that he was deprived of his marital rights. He has deceived his second wife by giving her a pledge of faith when that faith was bound to another, and behaving as if he were free to marry.

The woman who furnished the occasion for this adultery is no more free than her husband. For her to be silent when she sees him entering into an adulterous marriage is tantamount to endorsing it. Certainly she is guilty of a shameful pandering, since she willingly and knowingly let her husband prostitute himself in such a way.

What is the solution, then? Unless people are to be allowed to gain greater freedom to sin by sinning, each of them remains bound by the original pledge. The only way to solve the situation appears to be for the husband to acknowledge that he was an adulterer when he took a second wife before he was free to do so. The woman should acknowledge that she had a part in the crime or that, in fact, she was the primary source of the guilt.

If the man is unwilling to return to his former wife, there will be a strong suspicion of collusion, and the affair will furnish an evil and shameful example. I do not see that the woman who heedlessly made the divorce has the free right to marry again, unless she has offered to bring about a reconciliation.

What, then? Unless I am very much mistaken, the situation will have to stay perplexed. I do not know what to say unless the circumstances become better understood. I ask, distinguished sir, that you forgive my hesitancy if I do not venture to render a judgment between two people unknown to me, and in such a confused matter. Perhaps you expected something more of me, but I am sure that you will accept in good spirit what I have been able to say.

Farewell, honored brother. May the Lord always be with you, guide you with his Spirit of wisdom and uprightness, guard you with his protection, and sustain you with his virtue.

December 30, 1557.

PART VI

Judicial Questions

1. On Usury

The *CR* editors comment: "It is important to note that the word 'usury,' as employed by Calvin, does not have the same significance that we attach to the word today." No date is provided. Paul Henry, in *The Life and Times of John Calvin,* refers to the use of this letter at the national synod of Verteuil's 1567 meeting, at which it adopted "a great number of decisions of this kind" (pp. 468–469). Compare André Biéler, *La pensée économique et sociale de Calvin;* Lewis W. Spitz, ed., *The Reformation: Material or Spiritual?* and John H. Leith, *Calvin's Doctrine of the Christian Life.* See also P. E. Martin, "Calvin et le prêt à intérêt à Genève," in *Mélanges d'histoire économique et sociale en hommage Antony Babel* (Geneva, 1963), 251–263. [Pages 245–249]

From John Calvin to one of his friends.

I have not personally experienced this, but I have learned from the example of others how perilous it is to respond to the question for which you seek my counsel. For if we should totally prohibit the practice of usury, we would restrain consciences more rigidly than God himself. But if we permit it, then some, under this guise, would be content to act with unbridled license, unable to abide any limits.

If I were writing to you alone, I would have no fear of such a thing, for your prudence and the moderation of your heart are well known to me. But because you seek counsel for another, I fear that if I say anything he might permit himself more than I would prefer. Nonetheless, since I have no doubt that, in light of human nature and the matter at hand, you will thoughtfully consider the most expedient thing to do, I will share what I think.

First, there is no scriptural passage that totally bans all usury. For Christ's statement, which is commonly esteemed to manifest this, but which has to do with lending [Luke 6:35], has been falsely applied to usury. Furthermore, as elsewhere, when he rebukes the sumptuous guests and the ambitious invitations of the rich, he commands us to call instead the blind, the lame, and the other poor of the streets, who cannot repay. In so doing he corrects the world's vicious custom of lending money [only to those who can repay] and urges us, instead, to lend to those from whom no hope of repayment is possible.

Now we are accustomed to lending money where it will be safe. But we ought to help the poor, where our money will be at risk. For Christ's words far more emphasize our remembering the poor than our remembering the rich. Nonetheless, we need not conclude that all usury is forbidden.

The law of Moses [Deut. 23:19] is quite diplomatic, restraining us to act only within the bounds of equity and human reason. To be certain, it would be desirable if usurers were chased from every country, even if the practice were unknown. But since that is impossible, we ought at least to use it for the common good.

Passages in both the prophets and the Psalms display the Holy Spirit's anger against usurers. There is a reference to a vile evil [Ps. 55:12, Vulgate] that has been translated by the word *usura*. But since the Hebrew word *tok* can generally mean "defraud," it can be translated otherwise than "usury."

Even where the prophet specifically mentions usury, it is hardly a wonder that he mentions it among the other evil practices [Neh. 5:10]. The reason is that the more often usury is practiced with illicit license, the more often cruelty and other fraudulent activities arise.

What am I to say, except that usury almost always travels with two inseparable companions: tyrannical cruelty and the art of deception. This is why the Holy Spirit elsewhere advises all holy men, who praise and fear God, to abstain from usury, so much so that it is rare to find a good man who also practices usury.

The prophet Ezekiel [22:12] goes still further, for in citing the horrible case in which the vengeance of God has been kindled against the Jews, he uses the two Hebrew words *neshek* and *tarbith*—a form of usury so designated in Hebrew because of the manner in which it eats away at its victims. *Tarbith* means "to increase," or "add to," or "gain," and with good reason. For anyone interested in expanding his personal profit will take, or rather snatch, that gain from someone else. But undoubtedly the prophets only condemned usury as severely as they did because it was expressly prohibited for Jews to do. Hence when they rejected the clear commandment of God, they merited a still sterner rebuke.

Today, a similar objection against usury is raised by some

who argue that since the Jews were prohibited from practicing it, we too, on the basis of our fraternal union, ought not to practice it. To that I respond that a political union is different. The situation in which God brought the Jews together, combined with other circumstances, made commerce without usury apt among them. Our situation is quite different. For that reason, I am unwilling to condemn it, so long as it is practiced with equity and charity.

The pretext that both St. Ambrose and Chrysostom cite is too frivolous in my judgment, that is, that money does not engender money. Does the sea or the earth [engender it]? I receive a fee from renting a house. Is that where money grows? Houses, in turn, are products of the trades, where money is also made. Even the value of a house can be exchanged for money. And what? Is money not more productive than merchandise or any other possession one could mention? It is lawful to make money by renting a piece of ground, yet unlawful to make it from money? What? When you buy a field, is money not making money?

How do merchants increase their wealth? By being industrious, you answer. I readily admit what even children can see, that if you lock your money in a chest, it will not increase. Moreover, no one borrows money from others with the intention of hiding it or not making a profit. Consequently, the gain is not from the money but from profit.

We may therefore conclude that, although at first such subtleties appear convincing, upon closer examination they evaporate, since there is no substance to them. Hence, I conclude that we ought not to judge usury according to a few passages of scripture, but in accordance with the principle of equity.

An example ought to clarify the matter. Take a rich man whose wealth lies in possessions and rents but who has no money on hand. A second, whose wealth is somewhat more moderate—though less than the first—soon comes into money. If an opportunity should arise, the second person can easily buy what he wants, while the first will have to ask the latter for a loan. It is in the power of the second, under the rules of bargaining, to impose a fee on the first's goods until he repays, and in this manner the first's condition will be improved, although usury has been practiced.

Now, what makes a contract just and honest or unjust and dishonest? Has not the first fared better by means of an agreement involving usury by his neighbor than if the second had compelled him to mortgage or pawn his goods? To deny this is to play with God in a childish manner, preferring words over the truth itself. As if it were in our power, by changing words, to transform virtue into vice or vice into virtue. I certainly have no quarrel here.

I have said enough; you will be able to weigh this more diligently on your own. Nonetheless, I should hope that you will always keep in mind that what we must bring under judgment are not words but deeds themselves.

Now I come to the exceptions. For, as I said at the beginning, we must proceed with caution, as almost everyone is looking for some word to justify his intention. Hence, I must reiterate that when I approve of some usury, I am not extending my approval to all its forms. Furthermore, I disapprove of anyone engaging in usury as his form of occupation. Finally, I grant nothing without listing these additional exceptions.

The first is that no one should take interest [usury] from the poor, and no one, destitute by virtue of indigence or some affliction or calamity, should be forced into it. The second exception is that whoever lends should not be so preoccupied with gain as to neglect his necessary duties, nor, wishing to protect his money, disdain his poor brothers. The third exception is that no principle be followed that is not in accord with natural equity, for everything should be examined in the light of Christ's precept: Do unto others as you would have them do unto you. This precept is applicable every time. The fourth exception is that whoever borrows should make at least as much, if not more, than the amount borrowed. In the fifth place, we ought not to determine what is lawful by basing it on the common practice or in accordance with the iniquity of the world, but should base it on a principle derived from the Word of God. In the sixth place, we ought not to consider only the private advantage of those with whom we deal but should keep in mind what is best for the common good. For it is quite obvious that the interest a merchant pays is a public fee. Thus we should see that the contract will benefit all rather than hurt. In the seventh place, one ought not to exceed the rate that a country's public laws allow. Although this may not always suffice, for such laws quite often permit what they are able to correct or repress. Therefore one ought to prefer a principle of equity that can curtail abuse.

But rather than valuing my own opinion over yours, I desire only that you act in such a humane way that nothing more need be said on the matter. With that in mind, I have composed these thoughts more out of a desire to please you than out of any confidence of satisfying you. But owing to your kindness toward me, I know you will take to heart what I have offered.

[I commit you] to God, my most excellent and honored friend. May he preserve you and your family. Amen.

2. Ecclesiastical Benefices

The *CR* editors note: "This piece was apparently written after the death of the Duchess Jeanne de Longueville, Countess of Neuchâtel, deceased in 1543." For a more thorough elaboration of Calvin's view of benefices, see the *Institutes* 4.5.4–7 (2:1087ff.). [Pages 249–251]

As for my advice, which the brother has requested, concerning the benefice he holds as a gift from the deceased Countess, but which formerly belonged to the church of Neuchâtel, without going into a lengthy debate, here is what my conscience dictates, based on the grace God has given me.

First, insofar as he has become poor for the Word of God and the gospel's sake, it is neither repugnant nor unreasonable that he should be sustained by a benefice of the church. Where sound order and administration prevail, it is appropriate and just that a part [of the church's wealth] be applied to such use in order to support those who have been deprived of their substance or have otherwise become poor for the sake of witnessing to Jesus Christ. For this reason I see no wrong in his utilizing a benefice to support himself, realizing that God is assisting him by this means, having tested him in the loss that he earlier gave to God.

It is true that this form of donation is not an effective instrument of aid. But, as reason dictates, I would rather embrace the equity of the right than its formality. Morever, keep in mind that the princess, being in France at the time, dared not do other than she did. Seeing then that her gift was without vice, I am confident that he may use it in clear conscience according to God. For as I have said, such benefices may be justly applied toward the sustenance and upkeep of those who otherwise would be destitute and suffer loss for the sake of the gospel.

As for the benefice passing perpetually on to his inheritors, that is more difficult. Granted it is proper for a benefice to help him, for it to be perpetually drawn off in favor of his family creates perilous consequences, setting an example that is neither wise nor approved. Of course, it might be proper for his children to receive an advance, sufficient to assist them to begin to serve God. Even the church has done as much in cases where fathers have defaulted. Consequently, I would not want to condemn such gifts, as I see them as worthy means of withdrawing benefits and riches in order to help the poor, both now and in the future.

The fact is, it is a pernicious error that today, in many places where the gospel is preached, ecclesiastical benefices are doled out or used in a profane manner, without any regard for the end to which they were dedicated. And although many may not take it very seriously, it constitutes an abuse that God will reform if men fail to do so.

I understand the common excuse that is offered: that these benefices were given to monks and priests, out of superstition, for the purpose of holding masses and funerals, idolatries, and nurturing their indolence, etc. That is why all this should be abolished. Or still better, princes could assign them to their domain as was done in ancient times when inheritances were labeled "lapsed."

But that is not the point in God's eyes. For the Word of God teaches us the proper use of all goods dedicated to his honor. Even in the early church, there were holy ordinances that governed their usage, which the emperors approved.

Therefore, priests and monks, falsely usurping the church's teaching and using without proper titles what does not belong to them, as well as poorly administering what they improperly occupy, have not been able to satisfy, by their masses, what was correctly ordained and have even broken or destroyed what was established by the authority of God. For it has always been maintained that offerings sanctified to God cannot be profaned. For this reason, we charge monks and priests with sacrilege.

At the same time, while not serving the church, they have squandered possessions designated for true ministers. Moreover, they have devoured the substance of the poor and spent it in sumptuous wastefulness and in still more villainous ways.

Accordingly, it is the prince's duty to redirect such gifts and to use them as originally intended, rather than allowing them to continue to be used by those whom we justly rebuke. And if anyone, anywhere in the world, contradicts this, let him fear lest God take hold of him!

It is a grave matter to fall into God's hands. For whoever meddles with God's offerings in order to enrich himself will be astonished at the rate of his own diminution—two- to three-fold. For God will never permit such a monk to prosper for long. Therefore, so much the more ought we to esteem God's grace and his blessing than accursed riches, which are sought without realizing how they confound their possessors.

Finally, beyond the evil and present injury, we must consider the scandal we raise for unbelievers. For we gather in offerings with the gospel, while at the same time searching for ways to alter them, by fishing in troubled waters, as the proverb puts it. That is, we seek means of preying on the church's possessions, as if they were forms of booty.

In addition, we are setting a bad example for those who will come after us. For since God has shown us the grace to call us first to the knowledge of his Word, then all the more will we be guilty if we introduce vices that others follow, based on what we shall have done.

3. How a Faithful Judge and Counselor Ought to Deport Himself When He Is Commissioned to Adjudicate Between Two Plaintiffs Over a Benefice

The following document shows Calvin to be a knowledgeable student of the legal traditions of the times. Note his respect for legal institutions. See his discussion of a Christian's use of law courts in the *Institutes* 4.20.17 (2:1505ff.); also his Commentary on 1 Corinthians 6:1–8. [Pages 251–252]

The contents of M. Bartonnier's letter having been communicated to the Company of Pastors of this church, their will is to concur with him that all the faithful, insofar as they can, ought to shun all handling of things that either approve of or consent to the party of idolatries, or which in any way have to do with profaning things that ought to be consecrated for use in the true church, in order to uphold its legitimate order. Accordingly, in their view, a counselor who knows the truth of Jesus Christ ought to decline, at arm's length, such commissions as the letter in question describes, and leave them for others to decide.

Nevertheless, if a counselor finds himself so involved, not having perceived the difficulties such a case entails (but which experience would have foreseen), their advice is that he, in order to disentangle himself from as much evil as possible, affirm with a clear conscience that he cannot approve of such abuses and, being only an executor, cannot interject himself further into the matter.

As for those courts and judges before whom such matters come for debate, it is quite different. For a judge is no longer at liberty to decline, as a counselor may, since the judge is properly constituted to hear those public differences involving benefices, which, according to custom and the ordinances of the king, are uniquely his to adjudicate. Therefore, a judge, constrained to pronounce in such cases, should be advised to declare that, although neither the plaintiff nor the defendant has a well-established case, and that divine right favors neither party, nonetheless, in accordance with the laws of the Roman court, approved by the king, he must adjudicate within such bounds.

However, if a judge is able to find a means to refer these pleaders elsewhere, that would be far better for the sake of his conscience, as if he were availing himself of a substitute papist. And whether he send them to a civil court or a higher court, let him voluntarily surrender the case, thereby demonstrating on his part that he derives no satisfaction from stirring in such dung.

Beyond this, although the letter refers to other problems that are not specified, it is impossible to respond, except in generalities.

4. Response to a Question About the Annual Profit of the Papal Priesthood and the Value of the Sale

Commenting on the holding of financial gain from holding papal priesthoods, Calvin says it is not permissible to continue gaining from the ties with the Roman Catholic Church. Calvin advises the transfer of funds gained unjustly "as seems best."

On a second matter, Calvin says that an adolescent who married without parental consent must remain faithful even though his wife is defiant. [Pages 252–254]

If I must give advice on a matter which is still unsettled, I would say that I think it is not permissible to hold any priesthoods in the papacy, no matter how specious the pretext may be. Every penny collected from such priesthoods would be stained with sacrilege. However, if anyone has come away with a profit, out of ignorance and error, I do not see why he should be concerned to give it back. (I am distinguishing between a basic livelihood and great riches which he may have stored up; if a person has enriched himself from the latter, he is not free from anathema until he returns what he is keeping unjustly.) Just as Moses left the palace and luxury of Pharaoh with a tranquil conscience because he had not sought that sort of life of his own accord, so today, when a person removes himself from that accursed wealth with which he supported himself for a time, he can earn a living for himself by legitimate means in the future with a quiet mind.

As to the value of the sale, that agreement was undoubtedly accursed, but the buyer is dead, and the person who received the money unjustly cannot do anything except willingly transfer to someone else that wealth which has defiled him, as soon as he has the opportunity and occasion. He should distribute what he has kept as seems best, in accordance with his own judgment, so that he is not enriched at the expense of someone else.

When an adolescent has married without his parents' knowledge, he should recognize that he is paying a just penalty for his heedless behavior if his wife is unresponsive to him. He did not offer God and his parents the obedience he owed them, and he should not be surprised if he gets his just reward in the form of his wife's defiance. Because it is not disagreement over religion which is tearing the marriage apart, he should fulfill his marital duty as long as he can live with his wife without danger. If greater force and necessity compel him to leave her, he should remain celibate until his wife recovers her senses or gives him cause to divorce her.

                                        September 1, 1560.

PART VII

Miscellanies

1. A Response to Five Questions

Calvin addresses five separate issues: whether one should leave one's spouse over religious persecution; how to determine what mourning attire is appropriate; on the wisdom of not vying for the property of persons who have had to flee because of persecution; on the rectitude of assisting religious prisoners; and on the appropriateness of withholding Communion from those who have participated in the Mass. Charles d'Espeville was a name by which Calvin sometimes signed his letters. [Pages 255–258]

On the first question, concerning the extent to which the principle of leaving one's spouse, due to religious persecution, pertains, I always exhort the married not to leave their partner until they have tried everything within their power to attract and win the other, because the marriage bond merits our fulfillment of all its vows. Without a doubt, anyone who abandons his partner lightly, for other than religious scandals and their forseeable consequences, violates the bond he owes the other. If the husband or the wife who opposes the gospel permits his partner to worship God purely, I do not think it proper for either husband or wife to leave the other. Even if the faithful partner is prevented from worshiping God rightly, he or she ought still to use gentleness to soften the partner's heart. Hence, neither should leave without being under the restraint of grave peril, that is, unless the wife threatens her husband or he threatens her. This is the path conscience should take until persecution from elsewhere arises and necessitates a departure, for no divorce ought willingly to be sought.

What then? May those who have left their partners remarry? Such severances do not break the marriage bond; rather they provide flight from the fury of the gospel's enemies. He who has so retired must still earnestly solicit his partner until an evident cause for divorce is found. And those who are separated in this manner ought to live as widowed.

As for those whose partners have committed adultery, unless this can be verified, they must practice patience, for a divorce cannot be obtained in such cases without the cause being established. No matter what charges—however notorious—one might bring before a judge, the offended party must be able to provide information that will prove his case. Then, after hearing the delinquent party, if adultery is proven, even if no sentence is passed, a Christian church may proceed to marry those who can produce such hearings; otherwise, no.

On the second question, concerning mourning attire, I am unaware of any binding regulations. For in the first place, the matter is similar to other infirmities of a worldly order that we tolerate. Moreover, since it is not specifically required to suppress such things unless they become scandalous or offensive, too much rigor or austerity in these matters seems unwise. Nonetheless, everyone ought to be warned and exhorted to forgo superfluous pomp and vain foolishness. For anyone who has profited in the school of God will find no pleasure in such things and will utilize them only as a matter of duty, conforming to what is customary.

On the third question, concerning the wish to confiscate the property of those who are persecuted, that cannot be done without causing harm. For the letters that one would have to obtain to pursue one's case would contain obvious blasphemies against the honor of God, since false charges would have to be cited. And whoever would want to receive such property would have to produce what amounts to a form of deception, which would result in unparalleled evil. Consequently, I do not deem it proper for anyone instructed in the gospel to entangle himself in such deceptions. Nevertheless, if someone should want to obtain part of it for the gospel, I see no reason why this could not be done, provided the person involved not procure letters of opprobrium in the name of God or accept such, but withdraw what he can without participating in evil.

On the fourth question, concerning the rectitude of assisting prisoners, incarcerated for religious reasons, to escape, either by money or other means, I would not dare give such advice, nor approve of it. But whenever such escapes occur, I pray God that they will end well and I rejoice if I hear that the persons involved escape without harm or scandal.

In scripture, whenever the disciples were imprisoned, the church prayed for them rather than preferring some other action. Even St. Paul did not want to be ransomed by money. Accordingly, lest we err, the better course is to abstain from such practices. Nevertheless, when anyone escapes by such means, although I might not personally justify his deed, I praise God for his deliverance and support those who take such actions rather than condemn them.

On the last question, concerning how one ought to view those who return to idolatries after having participated in the Lord's Supper, it is certainly necessary to adopt some ordering procedure to bridle such abuses, and in this instance, as in all others, it is wise to take action. For on the one hand, we ought not to permit the Lord's Supper to be profaned without taking some corrective measure; yet, on the other, we do not want to be so strict as to discourage the weak.

For example: It would seem proper to deny the Lord's Supper to anyone who, the first time, leans again toward superstitions, provided he ceases to practice them or abandons those monstrous acts which make idolatry so heinous. Above all, such a person ought to be penitent. As for those who succumb a second or third time, the penalty should be more severe for several reasons. First, because by acceding to their weakness we would be nurturing their evil and ultimate perdition. And second, because, having exposed their mockery of God's name and the breaking of their promise, we would be condoning their license. Hence, in the end, instead of serving reverence, we would be contributing to evil.

Charles d'Espeville.

2. On Various Subjects

This is a circular letter written for several churches on several matters of order and discipline. Instruction and examination for participation in the Lord's Supper are to be undertaken. Those charged with pastoral disciplines should be kind and restrained, always leaving the way open for a defense to be made. The benefices of the papacy must be resigned. Those in the Reformed churches should not present their children for papist baptism or engage in prayers for the dead. Preaching, independent of the Reformed churches, ought to be permitted as a temporary measure if it is sound doctrine and does not become a substitute for ordinary church attendance. Assemblies organized by monks, and added ceremonies, should be avoided. Dice

games and cards, while not utterly contemptible, encourage bad
behavior and gambling and are better left alone. Pastors of Reformed churches and their families deserve the support of the
churches. Finally, Calvin issues a general admonition of peni-
tence against the attacks of the enemies of the faith. See Calvin,
"Draft Ecclesiastical Ordinances," in *Calvin: Theological Treatises*, trans. J. K. S. Reid, pp. 56–72; Robert Kingdon, "A Fresh
Look at Calvin's Attempt to Introduce Discipline Into a Reformed Community: The Consistory of Geneva 1542–1564," in
A. D. Pont, *Calvin–France–South Africa*. [Pages 258–262]

Dearest brothers, since this letter largely relates to individual
churches in your midst, we have decided that the most conven-
ient thing to do is to give you our letter to share. We are doing
this not so much to avoid labor as to avoid expending so many
words uselessly in individual letters, and especially to convince
you that we are not saying one thing in one letter and something else in another. We want our consensus to be made
known to all equally.

We hear that certain people are displeased when they are
questioned about their faith in order that, if they are found to
be poorly instructed in the faith, they may be denied admit-
tance to the Lord's Supper until they have made better progress. To those who are displeased by this strictness of yours, we
say that they should not indulge their wickedness or seek indulgence in a matter that concerns their destruction. The apostle's
opinion ought to be well known among Christians, that anyone
who eats the Lord's bread unworthily is considered sacrilegious
[1 Cor. 11:27]. For a person to use the bread worthily requires
that he should examine himself; the apostle teaches quite
clearly that those who are incapable of examining themselves
should not approach that table.

Anyone, therefore, who approaches the Lord's Supper heedlessly, without being instructed beforehand in the faith, arouses
God's anger. Those who are forbidden to approach it for this
reason have nothing to complain of, since their salvation is
being protected. If everyone were wise, everyone could be his
own judge; but because many pay too little attention to themselves, it is expedient that the church have a definite procedure
so that it never fails to prevent the sacraments from being
profaned.

For everyone to be admitted to the Lord's Supper, without

distinction or selection, is a sign of contempt that the Lord cannot endure. The Lord himself distributed the supper to his disciples only. Therefore anyone not instructed in the doctrine of the gospel ought not to approach what the Lord has instituted. No one should be distressed when his Christianity is examined even down to the finest point when he is to be admitted to the Lord's Supper. It should be established as part of the total state and system of discipline that ought to flourish in the church that those who are judged unworthy should not be admitted.

We know this seems novel to those who do not maintain a distinction between the yoke of our Lord Jesus Christ and the tyranny of the papacy, but it is your responsibility to search out the Lord's will and submit yourselves to it, rather than to relax the reins on your desires. Even the example of infidels may inspire us with shame. Granted that they did not show that reverence in their superstitions which we ought to show in the sacraments; they nevertheless acknowledged that those judged to be defiled by some crime should be kept away from their superstitious rites.

When the Lord's Supper is forbidden to someone, he should not think that he is excluded for all time, or that he has been thrown into a desperate situation. The purpose is for him to humble himself, and for others to learn through him. All this is set forth in the Word of God, and we ask of you through the Lord that you not be ashamed to subject yourselves in a matter that you know to be good and holy.

We are aware that you have among you men who have been chosen and appointed to correct scandals, to warn those who are sinful, and to acknowledge those who conduct themselves honorably. Those who are called to these responsibilities ought to show kindness and restraint, so that no one is slandered on the pretext of censure or pursued by false accusation, false denunciations, or suspicions. We touch on this particularly so that admonishing may be done in such a way that the person admonished has a chance to be heard, in case he has a defense to make, and so that no window is opened for slandering the innocent and causing them trouble. Each one therefore should be accused before the elders, in accordance with their responsibility. In this way, he may defend himself when charged, and if he is found innocent, his accuser may be corrected separately for being too careless. (If a wicked intent has led him to make the accusation, that would clearly be intolerable.) It is for you to beseech the Lord to guide with his Spirit those whom you have chosen for that responsibility, with true foresight, gentleness, zeal, and uprightness. You should let yourselves be restrained by those curbs which we all need, and let those who must examine others be the first to be corrected and punished themselves.

Among the faults which many people wish condoned in their behavior is this one: They ask that they may be allowed to keep the benefices of the papacy (as they call them), and to carry on business related to them. This must be condemned altogether, without any debate. For someone to defile himself with such sacrileges is clearly a crime inconsistent with Christianity.

Another matter of less consequence, outwardly, is the bringing of infants for a papist baptism, or attending papist funeral services. Those who want to be allowed to do this, or who at least do not want it charged against them as a sin, should examine themselves seriously and set God as judge before their eyes. When they do, they will readily pass judgment on themselves. You know the foul and detestable superstitions and even outright tricks of Satan that have defiled baptism in the papacy. Anyone who brings his infant for that sort of baptism defiles him (insofar as he can), and does not gain for him the Lord's blessing.

To take part in prayers made for the dead can only diminish the unique sacrifice of our Lord Christ, since purgatory depends only on human reparations. You should consider whether this is pardonable and whether, when someone has so scandalized the church, his action should be ignored or tolerated as a slight fault. Does this person not rather deserve the sort of censure that would warn him to be more careful in the future? We know the difficulties that are besetting you, and we sympathize with you in keeping with our duty of affection, but it does not help to be absolved by us. You should allow the judgment of God's Word to be brought against you so that everything may work toward your good and salvation.

We hear that another matter is being debated among you: whether someone should be allowed to put himself forward to preach in a place where there is a Reformed church, even if this has not been approved by the church, and, if a person has done this, whether people should be allowed to come and hear him preach. Please listen carefully to what we say. Although the Lord has established a certain body of the church among you there, in the state of general disorder that still prevails there you should tolerate many things which you would not tolerate in a well-established church. (We are not talking about those actions in which there is sin against God and which are inconsistent with his Word.) The wretched papists are like scattered sheep, and when the Lord calls forth certain men to gather them together from their scattered condition, we ought not to impede this help that is offered them. We should rather, in this case, adopt for ourselves that saying of the Lord that those who are not against us are for us [Luke 9:50].

We are not talking here about the position of a pastor, but only about the work of a person who teaches in such a way that he gradually draws to Christ those who have been scattered. We also are not talking about a permanent arrangement, but about an extraordinary, intermediate situation that the Lord is using in the disordered state of the papacy. You recall the apostle's saying, that those who are not within the church are not subject to its rule and statutes [1 Cor. 5:12], and we must respect what the same apostle says elsewhere, that it is a cause for rejoicing when the gospel is preached even "in pretense" [Phil. 1:18].

Therefore it does not seem to us that the faithful should be kept away from the preaching of these men, provided their doctrine is upright and pure. There should be no superstitious praying, however, or any other mixing in of superstitions. Also, the people should not take this as a chance to withdraw from their ordinary assembly, and they should not assemble with less enthusiasm to hear their regular pastor. On the contrary, they should be aroused and strengthened to keep the church order into which the Lord has led them. Be careful that you are not surrounded by those who may attempt to lead the sheep from the flock by a side path, and estrange them from their ordinary pastorate. It seems to us that these preachers should be tolerated, unless people are attracted to them by curiosity or by a turning away from the straight path.

It is a more serious matter that some are even attending the assemblies of the monks, and sprinkling the word of truth with their lies in order to win favor. As if we were not all too prone to vanity and lies ourselves, or needed to look for new teachers to guide us to them! The Lord rightly punishes those who are delighted by such mixing of different elements. It is clear that most of them have turned aside from the truth and are stained with Satan's false claims. Only their ingratitude causes this; they are not content with pure doctrine but want to feed on the wind, and the Lord, by a just judgment, allows them to become drunk.

Be careful that you are not among those who are always learning, as Paul says, but never attain the knowledge of truth [2 Tim. 3:7]. Be mindful of the Lord's admonition to beware of the leaven of the scribes and Pharisees; when we are imbued with it, it is hard to be cleansed of it, so that no filth sticks to us. What, then, will become of the people who want to live with them and deliberately test God?

The same applies to that whole class of added structures which they call "hours" and "paternosters," and to other similar instruments of idolatry. Idols should be an abomination to us; we should not even have their names in our mouths. See Psalm 16, verse 4, to which that passage in Ezekiel [36:32] corresponds; if we truly repent of our past lives and of the ways by which we have gone astray, we cannot fail to be ashamed of those ways.

There are other small corruptions too, dice games and what they call cards. I acknowledge that these do not have anything to do with superstitions, but they are instruments of other vices and have brought much loss and evil everywhere. We would not utterly condemn games of this sort if proper behavior had a place in them, but where is that sort of sobriety? Nothing else holds men stuck fast, as with sticky birdlime, the way these games do, or occupies their senses completely, so that they are virtually bewitched. Those who grow accustomed to the games cannot say goodbye to them, but on the other hand, a person who draws back from them a little will easily come to loathe them.

Those who surrender themselves to these games and continue with their insane behavior will fall into many other troubles. Games almost never take place without blaspheming, cheating, and fiery quarrels. Even families have been torn apart by them. No one observes moderation; everyone exhausts and gradually consumes himself. Especially when profit is made, God himself is almost certain to be injured in some way. Therefore it is expedient to stay away from these games as much as possible, and it is best to abstain from them altogether.

Please do not be offended when we say that some pastors of churches in your midst are burdened with large families, and that you should be concerned for their need. A pastor cannot devote himself totally to his duties with a free and calm mind when his family is in need and he has no way to help them. When we hear from God's word that we must support those who serve the church, this is not to be limited to the pastors themselves; they would not be human if they were not as concerned for their families as for themselves. We are doing what we can here, but there is such need that we are not able to relieve it. We have no doubt, though, that you will do your duty so well that you will not need the stimulus of our encouragement; it is enough for us to have pointed out this matter to you.

In closing, we ask you to struggle unceasingly, since we do not doubt that you are under attack every day from enemies of the faith. Do not relax until you have overcome all of Satan's attacks and have finished your course and come to the blessed final goal. Realize that you will be aided by heavenly defenses, namely, the assurance that we are going to be with the one who makes us worthy of the grace of being received into his protection. Therefore, let us possess our souls in patience. It is not right for us to conquer by violence, and you know how poorly it turns out when we make an attack rashly, without the Lord's command. It is a hard temptation, and it is difficult to overcome it when we see the impious raging against the innocent, but we must fix our gaze upon that to which we are called. Since it is the Lord's will that we should be afflicted for a cause of such importance, we should not be indifferent to it. We should strive instead to learn how greatly we should prefer to this frail life the glory of God, the obedience that we owe him, Christ's kingdom, and the hope of eternal life. Make use of what scripture teaches, that by renouncing yourself you are a sacrifice of sweet fragrance to the Lord.

We greet you heartily and entreat the Lord to look upon you

and free you from all your adversaries, guard you with his protection, guide you with his Spirit, and increase you with every good thing.

3. On Three Particular Subjects

Calvin comments on whether it is permissible for ministers to make a profit from their money; on exacting an oath in the consistory; and on admitting public officials to the consistory. He gives a qualified approval to ministers making a "fair and honest return." He says that the consistory may require an oath, if it avoids the appearance of civil judicial authority, and he accepts the participation of civil authorities in the consistory, provided that civil and ecclesiastical jurisdiction remain distinct. See W. Fred Graham, *The Constructive Revolutionary: John Calvin and His Socio-Economic Impact.* [Pages 262–263]

I would have been more diligent in answering, dearest brother, if I had not been held back by the difficulty that seemed to be connected with the question you ask in your letter. You ask whether it is permissible for ministers to exact and realize a profit on their money. If I say "no" categorically, my answer could be judged harsher than is right, and retorts might be made. Therefore I would not venture to state that it is not allowed. I know how likely this is to cause false accusations and scandals, however, and how most people stretch the limits of the possessions they are allowed to acquire, even under conditions of restraint, and I would much rather stop short of committing myself than to make a full reply and give as my opinion that this matter should be freed of restraint once and for all.

It would be wise, of course, to abstain from transactions of this sort and from grasping after profits. Jeremiah has a purpose in testifying about himself: "I have neither lent on usury, nor have men lent to me on usury, yet every one of them curses me" [Jer. 15:10]. When a minister of the Word can restrain himself from profit of this sort, he is making the right decision for himself. Nevertheless, it is more tolerable for him to realize that profit than to go into business himself or undertake some pursuit that would call him away from the duties of his office, and therefore I do not see that it merits condemnation as a general thing. I would like to see restraint used. He should not, of course, stipulate a definite rate of return, or that a specific amount of money should be paid out to him. He may, however, invest his money with an honest man whose good faith and honesty he can trust. He should be content with a fair and honest return on his money, in keeping with the manner of God's blessing upon him as the user of wealth.

On the matter of exacting an oath in the consistory, you must act prudently to counter the detractions and murmurings of the wicked. It will be best, therefore, if those who are called will swear an oath when there is a need for it, and will stand as if at God's tribunal, since God himself is presiding in such an assembly. You must carefully avoid any sort of action that has the appearance of jurisdiction, or even anything like it.

Finally, I do not see any difficulty in admitting to the consistory those who are in charge of normal, civil jurisdiction, provided they are not present because of the prestige and respect given their jurisdiction. A distinction should always be observed between those two clearly distinct areas of responsibility: civil and ecclesiastical. Aside from this, there is no reason to exclude them from our investigations and rulings on spiritual matters. In short, when suitable men have been chosen for that office, let them see to it that they not combine the power of the sword with something which, by its very nature, should remain distinct from that power.

I felt that I should answer your questions this way, but I do not want the answers to seem to have come only from my opinions. I have consulted my brothers about them expressly, and they have approved.

Farewell.
January 10, 1560.

4. On Certain Important Subjects

Calvin comments on lending money at interest, on whether a widow may keep her children and whether an abused wife may leave her husband. He says he cannot offer a definite rate, since even a legal rate may cause an undue burden on a poor person. His advice is to follow Jesus' summary of the law, "that we should not do to someone else what we would not want done to us." He urges that a widow be encouraged, if she can, to help her children, and that a woman whose safety is in danger from her husband should leave him for a time. [Pages 264–266]

In lending out money at interest, it frequently happens that things occur which go beyond what is right and fair. It is not safe for me, therefore, dearest brother, to give a simple answer to the question you put to me: What limit should be established on legitimate interest for money? Sometimes even the slightest interest cannot be collected without displeasing God and injuring a neighbor. I ask you to excuse me, therefore, if I do not prescribe anything definite, as you are expecting.

In this city a definite limit has been set by law. This does not mean, however, that a creditor should be allowed in good conscience to exact interest even up to that limit from a poor man, if the poor man is burdened in some way as a result.

I am prevented from replying to you fully for another reason, too: because I know you are only asking me this in order to convict a certain person who allows himself complete license in this area. I also know that you do not want me involved in this deliberation because the person would, perhaps, not be willing to listen to me. Therefore, let the rule of natural law give him an answer for me, that rule which the Lord Jesus Christ established as part of the summation of the law and the prophets: that we should not do to someone else what we would not want done to us.

As to what you ask about the widow, if she is able to take her children away with her, nothing should be more precious to her than their souls. If the Lord has stretched out his hand to her, therefore, so that she is able to emerge from that mire (or rather, that abyss), she will not act humanely, and certainly not in a properly Christian way, if she leaves them behind. However, it is not clear to me what her age is, or her inclination, or the resources she has for acting properly; I leave it up to her to consider these matters individually. Whatever the case may be, she cannot leave them behind of her own accord without knowing that she will bring herself unending sorrow.

The case of the married woman is more difficult. I cannot approve her leaving her husband unless she is driven to it by some extreme violence, or if her husband, on the pretext of religion or some other excuse, is treating her in an intolerable manner. I will not define that intolerable manner, either, since she may be treated even more harshly at home. She ought to show every degree of tolerance before resorting to that remedy.

If she cannot be safe from idolatry except by clearly endangering her life, and if her husband presses her to such an extent that he actually persecutes her himself, then she will be permitted to take thought for herself and flee. Her intent should not be to turn away from her husband and desert him, however harsh and intolerable he may have shown himself to be, but only to avoid obvious danger, and only until the Lord causes her husband's savage heart to grow mild and calm. It is wrong to sin against God to please any mortal.

You are greatly concerned for others, but I hope you will, all the more, consider your duty toward that great heavenly Father by whom you have been endowed with the light of the gospel of his Son, in which our salvation rests. You have made a good beginning, but you must all the more strive earnestly in the future, every day and by every means, to continue your progress. Since so many small corruptions flourish there, you must be careful not to think that you can carry out your responsibility in any other way than by being eager for God's name to be glorified, and for his worship and honor to flourish among you as they should.

May the Lord be prevailed upon by my prayers, and bring about what I am asking of you in his name.

April 28, 1556.

Appendix I
Calvin's "Essay on the Lord's Supper" from *The For of Prayers,* 1542 and 1545.

See also Calvin's "Short Treatise on the Lord's Supper," in *Calvin: Theological Treatises,* trans. J. K. S. Reid; and Elsie Anne McKee, *John Calvin on the Diaconate and Liturgical Almsgiving,* pp. 50ff. [*CR* 34:193–196]

The Eucharist is the communion of the body and blood of the Lord. As St. Paul explains, it ought to be taken in order that we might abide and live more fully in Christ and he might live and abide more fully in us. For this reason St. Paul stresses that in the celebration of the Holy Supper we ought increasingly to desire to live and abide in Christ (i.e., to eat the flesh and drink the blood of the Lord) and to receive this meat and drink with greater fruitfulness and religious fervor. Hence, it is necessary to institute and to control this sacrament in order that the people might be duly instructed and admonished as to the necessity of their frequent participation in the flesh and blood of the Lord as well as to its great benefits, which are received from this participation and mastication.

From this it follows, first, that the Supper ought only to be offered to those who are willing and able to live in the Lord, who have him living in them, and who desire that his life be increased and made greater in them. For the reason why the communion of the body and blood of Christ is given in the Holy Supper is to the end that we might live entirely in him and he in us. Consequently, it is necessary for God's faithful ministerial dispensers to know that those to whom they wish to give the Lord's Supper are already incorporated by baptism into the Lord Christ, knowing that they are his true and living members, and that they hunger for this meat of eternal life and thirst for this holy drink. Christian charity, religion, and holy administration have always required this. Other persons, be-use they cannot participate in the sacrament without condemning themselves, must be kept away from the Holy Supper by the deacon (as the early church commanded). This is true also for those who have not yet been fully instructed in the Christian religion, the wicked, and those who have had to leave the church and who should be making penance, but who have not yet been received in grace. For this reason our Lord himself gave the first supper only to those more elect disciples. It is not fitting to give what is holy to dogs nor to give the meat of eternal life to those who do not hunger for it.

Therefore the Lord's Supper should only be given to those who are known and approved by the rule of charity and religion, a rule which must be practiced in the administration of the Supper, also requiring confession and the acknowledgment that, in our life, nothing contradicts it. Ministers, therefore, act in a holy and correct manner, both by their ministry and by its dignity, when they receive only those persons to the sacrament whom they first of all know to be approved and instructed. Moreover, since this meat and drink of eternal life ought to be administered only to those who truly desire it, it follows that the people to whom the Supper is administered should be admonished so thoroughly as to understand how important it is for them to profit from communion with Christ and what benefits are offered in it to them.

For this reason we begin, quite rightly, the mystery of the Supper by confessing our sins. Then we add the reading of the law and the gospel with psalms, in order that by the confession of our sins and the explication of the divine law (which assigns present and eternal punishment for sins but retains present and eternal rewards for the good) we might be drawn by a greater understanding and sentiment from our sins, realizing that they are the cause of eternal damnation.

For when we consider how opposed our entire life is to the law of God, that not a single work of ours is good, and that sin still exercises a great dominion in our flesh, such that we do not do the good we want but the evil we hate, we acknowledge how necessary it is for the communion of the body and blood of the Lord to be increased in us. For only Christ's flesh and blood possess righteousness and life. There is nothing good in our flesh and blood that can inherit the kingdom of God. Thus, it is appropriate in the Holy Supper that, in addition to the confession of our sins, we pray for forgiveness, read and explicate the divine law, and sing psalms, magnifying the majesty of God, expounding the law, and asking God for forgiveness.

Now, since we know, through the preaching of the gospel, that Jesus Christ our Lord—who is true God and true man—has, by means of the cross, satisfied his Father for our sins by this oblation of his body and blood, and that by our participation in them it has pleased God to make it possible for us to live in Christ and him in us, we realize all the more what excellent benefits are offered to us in the communion of the body and blood of the Lord.

First, we are assured of the remission of our sins and are confident of the grace of the Father, who has adopted us as his children and heirs, and who by his Son pardons all our iniquity, both original and present sin. Moreover, he pardons our sins every time we sin against him and humbly ask him for forgiveness. From this it follows that we may have confidence in the paternal benevolence and care of God in all adversity and may call upon him all the more boldly, asking all things from him that is good.

Next we are assured that as Jesus Christ is righteous and possesses life in himself, living for the Father who has sent him and giving to his followers the life of God—a life which indeed is happy and eternal—in order that they may live in him and he in them, so we learn that in the communion of the flesh and blood of Jesus Christ, we shall always enjoy more abundant life and righteousness from God, the only sure happiness. For to the extent that he makes it possible for us to live in him and he in us, who possess nothing good in ourselves, the more fully do we participate in his life, which is the life of God, full of righteousness and happiness.

Furthermore, by this same Jesus Christ, we are made righteous and live in new life because of him. Hence, in order that we might consider these things with greater diligence and be rendered more ardent and desirous of receiving his holy meat and drink of eternal life, we rightly sing psalms and hymns of praise, read the gospel, recite the confession of faith, and offer those holy oblations and gifts which testify to what has been given to us in Christ and witness to the benefits we have received by the communion of his flesh and blood. At least, they admonish us to esteem these things correctly and to laud them with true praises and ardent actions of thanksgiving, and to make them praiseworthy and precious among ourselves.

The truth of the matter is, there are good reasons for making such offerings. For when we (excited and moved by the reading and exposition of the gospel and the confession of our faith, which we do next) recall to mind that Jesus Christ is given to us from the infinite bounty of the heavenly Father and with him all things: i.e., the remission of sins, the covenant of eternal salvation, the life and righteousness of God, and finally all those desirable things which are added to the children of God, that is, to those who seek his kingdom and his righteousness, it is with good and just cause that we submit ourselves wholly to God the Father and to our Lord Jesus Christ, acknowledging so many and so great benefits. And we testify to this by giving offerings and holy gifts (as Christian charity requires), to Jesus Christ, which we do by giving them to the least, that is to say, to those who are hungry, who are thirsty, who are naked, who are strangers, who are sick, and who are held in prison. For all those who live in Christ and have him abiding in them will voluntarily do what the law commands. For the law commands that we do not come before God without an offering. We are also shown the same in that no one can be said to be subject to his earthly master, or to his benefactor, without acknowledging him with a gift.

Third, it follows that we ought to pray for the salvation of all men, since the life of Jesus Christ ought to be greatly aflame and vigorous in us. For the life of Christ consists in this: to seek and to save the lost. With good reason, therefore, we pray for all conditions of men.

Now because we truly receive Jesus Christ in this sacrament, with good cause we adore him in spirit and truth and receive the Eucharist with great reverence; then we conclude this mystery with praises and actions of thanksgiving. Hence the entire service and reason for administering the Supper is plain to us from the nature and institution of the Supper, which is also in accord with the manner of administration observed in the early church of the apostles, martyrs, and holy fathers, with whom we are equally in accord by administering all the sacraments in the common and vernacular tongue. For everything that is said pertains to everyone present, and must confirm and arouse our faith and inflame our desire for God in all things.

In addition, when admonishing the people to prepare themselves before coming to this sacred banquet, we further teach and admonish them the following four things.

First: We are so lost because of Adam's sin and our own that there is no one who is good in himself, neither in all our nature nor in all our flesh. Accordingly, neither our flesh nor blood can inherit the kingdom of God. From this it follows that we ought to be moved to acknowledge our sins and to break away from our evil life, in order that we might with a true heart confess our offenses and ask forgiveness for them.

Second: Jesus Christ alone is the one who has won the remission of our sins and obtained our pardon from the Father by his death and the pouring out of his precious blood. He also quickens his righteousness in us when he makes us live in him and when he lives in us.

Third: Christ takes part himself in this sacrament of the Supper, for in giving the bread and the wine he said, "Take and eat, this is my body, etc." Hence, he truly gives his body with the bread and his blood with the cup. Why? For the remission of sins and the confirmation of the new testament. For he says, "This is given for you." And later, "This is poured out for you for the remission of sins." And still again, "This is the new testament and the covenant of eternal grace," in order that, through Jesus Christ, God might be our true father and we his children. Hence, Jesus Christ gives himself in this sacrament in order that he might live in us and we in him; and thereby, because of his love, we are assured of the remission of our sins and the confirmation of the new covenant, in order that we might be the children of God and he our father. Thus we become one of the same race, same mind, and same nature. And if anyone refuses to acknowledge this, the Lord Jesus Christ will pray for him. For we need not doubt the word of Jesus Christ, his actions, or his power. For in this sacrament, Jesus gives us his body and his blood, to the end that we might live in him and he in us, assuring us that through him we have the complete abolishment of our sins, the confirmation of our heavenly Father's grace and eternal covenant, that we are the children of God, that he is our father, and that he gives us all good things.

Now herein two benefits accrue to us. The first is terrestrial, being the bread and wine. The second is celestial, which is the communion of Christ, i.e., his body and his blood. And these two things are given to us for two reasons: for the remission of our sins and the augmentation of Christ's life in us, which is the confirmation of the new covenant.

Finally, we teach that we ought to give thanks to the Lord Jesus for these great benefits with our hearts, our words, and our actions, and that we ought greatly to praise and exalt the memory of Jesus Christ and all his benefits, i.e., his incarnation, passion, resurrection, ascension, the sending of the Holy Spirit, his coming to judge the world, and, lastly, all those things he has done for us as well as appointed us to do.

Hence, in leaving behind all frivolous disputations and debates, we attempt to do and seek in the Supper primarily what we have said above, doing so that we might come to understand how necessary it is for Christ to live in us and we in him, to the end that we might believe that, in this sacrament, he so gives us himself that we might live in him and he in us. And this he does for the purpose of obtaining the remission of our sins and fulfilling the life of God in us, and also for pardoning our lack of any good. In sum, the principal thing about the sacrament's mystery is that we might live in Christ and he in us. This the heavenly Father grants us through Christ. Amen.

One should note that the Sunday before the Supper is celebrated, one announces it to the people: First, in order that each might prepare and dispose himself to receive it correctly, and with such reverence as befits it. Second, that children should not be presented unless they have been instructed and have made their profession of faith in the church. Third—in case there might be strangers who are uninstructed, in order that they might present themselves for instruction in the particulars—on the day that the Supper is celebrated, the minister touches on it toward the end of his sermon, or still better, makes it the subject of his entire sermon, in order to explain what our Lord wishes to say and signify by this mystery and in what way he wants it to be received.

Appendix II

A Copy of the Inquisitor Horris's Paper, Given to Those at Lyons Who Were Imprisoned for Preaching the Word, to Be Transmitted to M. Jean Calvin

The *CR* editors are unable to provide helpful footnotes to accompany this letter. It appears to be a copy of a certain Matthew Horris's interpretation of the supremacy of the gospel over law. Calvin's reply to this paper appears on pages 76–80 above. [*CR* 38/I:197–199]

I request that you write your Lordship and prevail upon him to see that the commandments of the old law are not the commandments given to Christians.

First, wherever another law exists, there other commandments exist. In the New Testament there exists another law, which we call "evangelical," which is not contained in the Old Testament, whose law is called "Mosaic." Hence the commandments given to Christians are different from those given to the Israelites.

Second, Christians are not required to observe commandments that are not [deemed] moral, i.e., based on natural or evangelical law, or based on the law of faith, which reflect the two orders of life, i.e., the human and the divine. The first pertains to man insofar as he is human; the second pertains to man insofar as he is Christian. Hence, any commandment that is not derived from the law of nature, i.e., from natural reason, or from faith, carries no obligatory force, even if it is written in the Old Testament.

Third, the precept given to ancient Israel forbidding the making and worshiping of graven images does not derive from natural reason. Consequently, it is not a moral precept nor does it belong to the law, for it appears neither in the gospel nor in the New Testament. Instead, it was a precept given specifically to the people of Israel to preserve them from idolatry, toward which they were strongly inclined and led by the example of the Gentiles, among whom they lived.

In the first place it is clearly evident that the precept in question is not a moral one. For it is not contrary to reason to speak through images and signs as God often did when he spoke to the prophets and saints of both Testaments. And through diverse similitudes he wished to represent for us distant things. Consequently, as it is not contrary to reason to teach one's neighbor by means of word or scripture, neither is it contrary to reason to teach him by means of representative images and similitudes. Certainly God did so. Hence, it is equally appropriate for us to do the same.

Moreover, God commanded them to set up two corporeal images of cherubim in the Temple to represent him and charged them to worship Abraham. And in the Apocalypse he appears in the image and similitude of the son of man.

For this reason we bow our heads when one reads the name of God and we hear the mystery of grace proclaimed, which is represented for us in the words of the sacraments. Likewise we kiss the Gospels, since they signify divine truth; also, we bow our heads and kiss, in an act of veneration, images, insofar as they represent the holy things that the divine words and Holy Scriptures signify. For all three, i.e., words, scripture, and images, are no more than holy signs. That is to say, their sanctity does not lie in their own being, as pagans thought was true of their idols, but it lies only in their capacity to signify the holy things they represent.

Furthermore, this precept neither derives from the law of faith nor is commanded by Jesus Christ and his Spirit in the New Testament. Consequently, those who wish to keep the old commandments judaize and renounce the faith, solemnly affirming by their action that Jesus Christ did not abolish the old law by his death—which is contrary to the scriptures of the New Testament.

Even more so are these judaizers guilty of grave error when they think that Exodus 20 contains our law's commandments and accordingly print them or inscribe them on their columns, proposing them as commandments given to Christians. For the scriptures teach us that the commandments of Exodus 20 are the old precepts and those of the gospel are the new. And the motive of inspiration behind the old commandments consists in temporal rewards and fear of punishment, as in being taken from Egypt and being beaten and punished unto the third and fourth generation of those who fail to keep them. Whereas the motive behind the commandments of the New Testament is the love of God and the love of eternal gain.

For this reason we have not received anew a spirit of bondage and of fear but a filial spirit in order to accomplish the law of grace in love. And whereas the old are fulfilled in accordance with reason and the law of Moses, the new are fulfilled in accordance with evangelical faith and love.

Therefore, there is as much difference between the two types of commandments as there is between Adam and Jesus and between a human man and a Christian man. Hence, Jesus Christ said that he gives us a new commandment containing new ordinances.

Moreover, those who limit themselves to the "letter" of what is written in Exodus 20 and of the other passages containing the old law necessarily confound and confuse the ceremonial with its moral use. Hence, they judaize and keep the decalogue of the Old Testament, thinking they are living a Christian life and keeping the decalogue of the New Testament. For in the Old Testament text it is written that one ought to keep the Sabbath and not make an altar of stone, and then only of earth without steps, and other such things which are written in the "letter" of the decalogue of Moses, and all of that is transplanted into the evangelical decalogue, given by Jesus Christ, and expressly placed into the Gospels and writings of the New Testament.

Bibliography

Reference is made to Calvin's *Institutes* by book, chapter, and section. Quotations of titles or text are from the McNeill-Battles translation, and references by volume and page number are to that translation. *CR* refers to the *Corpus Reformatorum.* At the end of each introductory paragraph, in brackets, is a reference to the pages in the *Corpus Reformatorum,* volume 38, part I, from which the document is translated.

Works by John Calvin

Calvin: Institutes of the Christian Religion. Edited by John T. Mc-Neill, trans. Ford Lewis Battles. Library of Christian Classics. 2 vols. Philadelphia: Westminster Press, 1960.

Calvin: Theological Treatises. Translated by J. K. S. Reid. Library of Christian Classics. Philadelphia: Westminster Press, 1954.

Calvin's New Testament Commentaries. Edited by David W. Torrance and Thomas F. Torrance. 12 vols. Edinburgh and London, 1959–68; Grand Rapids: Wm. B. Eerdmans Publishing Co., 1963–74.

Calvin's Commentaries. Calvin Translation Society edition. 47 vols. Edinburgh, 1843–59; reprint, Grand Rapids: Wm. B. Eerdmans Publishing Co., 1948–50.

"The Form of Church Prayers" [= "The Form of Prayers," 1542 and 1545]. In Bard Thompson, *Liturgies of the Western Church.* Cleveland and New York: World Publishing Co., 1961.

Ioannis Calvini Opera quae supersunt omnia. 59 vols. Edited by G. Baum, E. Cunitz, and E. Reuss. In *Corpus Reformatorum,* vols. 29–87. Braunschweig and Berlin, 1863–1900.

John Calvin's Sermons on the Ten Commandments. Translated by Benjamin W. Farley. Grand Rapids: Baker Book House, 1978.

Letters of John Calvin. Edited by Jules Bonnet. Vols. 1–2, trans. David Constable. Edinburgh, 1855–57. Vols. 3–4, trans. M. R. Gilchrist. New York, 1858. 4 vols., Philadelphia, 1858. Reprint, New York: Burt Franklin, Publisher, 1972–73.

"Project d'ordonnance sur les mariages." *Corpus Reformatorum* 38/I: 33–34, 105–114.

Tracts and Treatises. Translated by Henry Beveridge. 3 vols. Vol. 1, *On the Reformation of the Church.* Reprinted with an Introduction by Thomas F. Torrance. Grand Rapids: Wm. B. Eerdmans Publishing Co., 1959.

Other Books and Articles

Baldwin, Claude-Marie. "Marriage in Calvin's Sermons." In Robert Schnucker, ed., *Calviniana: Ideas and Influence of John Calvin.* Kirksville, Mo.: Sixteenth Century Publishers, 1988.

Battles, Ford Lewis. "Against Luxury and License in Geneva: A Forgotten Fragment of Calvin." *Interpretation* 19 (April 1965): 182–202.

Benoit, Daniel. "Weihnachten in Genf im Jahre des Heils 1550." In *Regards contemporains sur Jean Calvin.* Paris, 1965.

Biéler, André. *La pensée économique et sociale de Calvin.* Geneva: Librairie de l'Université, 1959.

Eire, Carlos M. N. "Calvin and Nicodemism: A Reappraisal." In *Sixteenth Century Journal* 10/1 (1979).

———. *War Against the Idols: The Reformation of Worship from Erasmus to Calvin.* New York: Cambridge University Press, 1986.

Graham, W. Fred. *The Constructive Revolutionary: John Calvin and His Socio-Economic Impact.* Richmond: John Knox Press, 1971; reprint, East Lansing, Mich.: Michigan State University Press, 1987.

Henry, Paul. *The Life and Times of John Calvin.* New York: Robert Carter & Brothers, 1851.

Kingdon, Robert. "A Fresh Look at Calvin's Attempt to Introduce Discipline Into a Reformed Community: The Consistory of Geneva 1542–1564." In A. D. Pont, *Calvin–France–South Africa.* Pretoria, 1990.

Leith, John H. *Calvin's Doctrine of the Christian Life.* Louisville, Ky.: Westminster/John Knox Press, 1989.

McKee, Elsie Anne. *John Calvin on the Diaconate and Liturgical Almsgiving.* Geneva: Librairie Droz, 1984.

Seeger, Cornelia. *Nullité de mariage, divorce et séparation de corps à Genève.* Lausanne: Société d'histoire de la Suisse romande, 1989.

Spitz, Lewis W. *The Reformation: Material or Spiritual?* Boston: D. C. Heath & Co., 1962.

Williams, George Huntston. *The Radical Reformation.* Philadelphia: Westminster Press, 1962.

Indexes

Scripture Index

General Index